SANS Step-by-Step Series

OpenSSH

A Survival Guide for Secure Shell Handling

Version 1.0

Secure Shell has been a long time coming. This replacement for clear-text passwords has been available for over a decade and yet you still see telnet, the r-utilities, and FTP in common use. The author and editor team sincerely hope this book helps increase the adoption rate of this most sensible protocol.

Tyler Hudak
Brad Sibley

June 2003

Document Legalities

Copyright © 2003, The SANS Institute. All rights reserved. The entire contents of this publication are the property of the SANS Institute. User may not copy, reproduce, distribute, display, modify or create derivative works based upon all or any portion of this publication in any medium whether printed, electronic or otherwise, without the express written consent of the SANS Institute. Without limiting the foregoing, user may not reproduce, distribute, re-publish, display, modify, or create derivative works based upon all or any portion of this publication for purposes of teaching any computer or electronic security courses to any third party without the express written consent of the SANS Institute.

Publication Designer: David Garrison
International Standard Book Number: 0-9724273-8-4
Library of Congress Control Number: 2003108410
Printed in the United States of America

Warning and Disclaimer

Every effort has been made to make this book as complete and as accurate as possible, but no warranty of fitness is implied. The information provided is on an "as is" basis. The authors and the publisher shall have neither liability nor responsibility to any person or entity with respect to any loss or damages arising from the information contained in this book.

Table of Contents

Disclaimer ... 4
Tell Us What You Think ... 4
Author Bios ... 5
Introduction ... 6
Foreword – Selling OpenSSH to Management ... 7
SECTION I - OBTAINING, COMPILING AND HANDLING OpenSSH ... 11
   Step 1.1 Install OpenSSH to Replace the Remote Access Protocols with Encrypted Versions ... 11
      Action 1.1.1   Download and install the GNU C compiler ... 11
      Action 1.1.2   Download, compile and install Zlib compression library ... 12
      Action 1.1.3   Download, compile and install a random number generator ... 13
      Action 1.1.4   Download, compile and install OpenSSL ... 15
      Action 1.1.5   Download, compile and install OpenSSH ... 16
      Action 1.1.6   Configure the sshd_config configuration file ... 17
      Action 1.1.7   Configure auto-start of sshd daemon (for OpenSSH server) ... 18
   Step 1.2 Install SSH Windows Clients to Access Remote Machines Securely ... 19
      Action 1.2.1   Download and install PuTTY for Windows ... 19
      Action 1.2.2   Download and install WinSCP - a graphical SSH file transfer tool ... 21
SECTION II – HOW TO USE OpenSSH CLIENTS FOR UNIX-TO-UNIX CONNECTIVITY ... 23
   Step 2.1 Use the OpenSSH Tool Suite to Replace Clear-Text Programs ... 23
      Action 2.1.1   Use OpenSSH as a replacement for telnet/rsh/rlogin ... 24
      Action 2.1.2   Use the sftp command as a replacement for FTP to exchange files with a remote system ... 24
      Action 2.1.3   Use the scp command as a replacement for "rcp" to exchange files with a remote system ... 27
      Action 2.1.4   Use of Unix .rhosts / .shosts files for OpenSSH host-based authentication ... 29
      Action 2.1.5   Verify the SSH encryption ... 32
SECTION III – HOW TO USE PuTTY/WinSCP FOR PC-TO-UNIX CONNECTIVITY ... 38
   Step 3.1 Use PuTTY as a Graphical Replacement for telnet and rlogin ... 38
      Action 3.1.1   Configure PuTTY to connect to a remote machine ... 38
   Step 3.2 Use PuTTY / plink as a Command Line Replacement for telnet / rlogin ... 41
      Action 3.2.1   Create an SSH session from the command line using PuTTY ... 41
      Action 3.2.2   Using Plink to initiate an SSH session from the command line or a script ... 42
   Step 3.3 Use WinSCP as a Graphical Replacement for FTP and RCP ... 44
      Action 3.3.1   Use WinSCP to connect to a remote machine ... 44
   Step 3.4 Use PuTTY's Tools to Transfer Files from the Windows Command Line ... 47

Action 3.4.1	Interactively transfer files from the command line with PSFTP ... 47
Action 3.4.2	Transfer files from the command line with PSCP ... 51

SECTION IV – USING PUBLIC KEY AUTHENTICATION ... 53

Step 4.1 Authentication with Public Keys ... 53
Step 4.2 Passphrase Considerations ... 53
Step 4.3 How to Generate a Key Pair Using OpenSSH ... 54

Action 4.3.1	Generating your public/private key-pair ... 54
Action 4.3.2	Configuring remote hosts to authenticate with your public key ... 56
Action 4.3.3	Using your public key for authentication to a remote server ... 57
Action 4.3.4	Removing your public/private keys ... 59

Step 4.4 How to Generate a Key Using PuTTY ... 60

Action 4.4.1	Generating a public / private key pair with PuTTY ... 60
Action 4.4.2	Setting up public key authentication ... 62
Action 4.4.3	Using PuTTY to log in with public key authentication ... 63
Action 4.4.4	Use public key authentication from the command line PuTTY tools ... 65
Action 4.4.5	Removing your public/private keys ... 65

Step 4.5 How to use OpenSSH Passphrase Agents ... 65

Action 4.5.1	Use ssh-agent and ssh-add to store your private keys in memory ... 66
Action 4.5.2	Verify the private keys are in memory ... 67
Action 4.5.3	Using ssh-agent to automatically log in to a remote machine ... 67
Action 4.5.4	Removing private keys from memory ... 67
Action 4.5.5	Shutting down ssh-agent ... 67

Step 4.6 How to use PuTTY Passphrase Agents ... 67

Action 4.6.1	Use Pageant to store your private keys in memory ... 67
Action 4.6.2	Verify Pageant has your private key stored ... 69
Action 4.6.3	Using Pageant to automatically log in to a remote machine ... 70
Action 4.6.4	Using Pageant with command line tools ... 70

Step 4.7 Using Public Key Authentication for Automated File Transfers ... 71

Action 4.7.1	Decide who trusts who ... 71
Action 4.7.2	Generate a key pair ... 71
Action 4.7.3	Copy the public key to the remote system ... 72
Action 4.7.4	Verify that you are able to log in without an authentication prompt ... 74
Action 4.7.5	Verify that a scp transfer works ... 74
Action 4.7.6	Secure the connection ... 74

SECTION V – TROUBLESHOOTING SSH CONNECTIONS 76
Step 5.1 General Troubleshooting 76
Action 5.1.1 Verify download and installation/configuration of software 76
Action 5.1.2 Verify OpenSSH commands are in the UNIX search path 78
Action 5.1.3 Utilize verbose option to OpenSSH commands 78
Action 5.1.4 Utilize OpenSSH server daemon log 80
Step 5.2 Troubleshooting Common OpenSSH Errors/Problems 83
Action 5.2.1 Receiving "Connection refused" error when attempting to connect 84
Action 5.2.2 Receiving "permission denied" error when attempting to connect using standard UNIX authentication 84
Action 5.2.3 Receiving password prompt when expecting public key passphrase prompt 84
Action 5.2.4 Getting immediate disconnect when attempting connection 85
Action 5.2.5 Passphrase is no longer valid and you know you didn't change it 86
Action 5.2.6 Unexpected Host Key not cached 86
Action 5.2.7 Cached Host Key does not match 87

SECTION VI – ADVANCED SSH TOPICS 88
Step 6.1 Port Forwarding 88
Action 6.1.1 Use OpenSSH to set up port forwarding 89
Action 6.1.2 Verify port forwarding is working 89
Action 6.1.3 Set up Pine to send and retrieve email through an SSH tunnel 90
Action 6.1.4 Use Pine to retrieve email using port forwarding 90
Action 6.1.5 Use Pine to send email using port forwarding 90
Step 6.2 Using Port Forwarding Within PuTTY to Read your E-mail Securely 91
Action 6.2.1 Configure the initial PuTTY settings required for port forwarding 91
Action 6.2.2 Configure IMAP port forwarding 91
Action 6.2.3 Configure SMTP port forwarding 92
Action 6.2.4 Create and verify the SSH connection and port forwarding 93
Action 6.2.5 Configure your email client 95
Step 6.3 X11 Forwarding 97
Action 6.3.1 Utilize the OpenSSH X11 forwarding feature to run X-Windows applications through a secure channel 97
Action 6.3.2 Utilize the X11 forwarding feature in PuTTY to run X-Windows applications through a secure channel 100

Conclusion 100
Appendix — Sample sshd_config file with extensive comments 101
Glossary 113

DISCLAIMER

SSH as used in this publication refers to Secure Shell in general or the protocol, and does not constitute an endorsement of the commercial products developed and distributed by SSH Communications Security.

TELL US WHAT YOU THINK

As you read this book, keep in mind your insights are most important to us. We value your opinion and appreciate any words of wisdom you're willing to share with us.

Please feel free to contact the SANS Institute at openssh@sans.org and be sure to include the book's title and authors as well as how we may contact you.

We will carefully review your comments and share them with the authors and editors who worked on the book.

SANS Institute
openssh@sans.org

Author Bios

Tyler Hudak

Tyler joined the computer industry working as a UNIX* and NT Systems Administrator with a small insurance company in Akron, Ohio. He later expanded his experience through several systems administration positions giving him experience in a wide variety of platforms and OS variants. This gave him the low-level technical expertise critical in the area of Information Security. Tyler has earned a B.S. in Computer Science from the University of Akron and is GCIA certified.

Currently, Tyler is employed by a national trucking company as a Network Security Analyst where he deals with all aspects of Information Security on a variety of systems. In his free time, Tyler likes to play with his daughters, watch B-movies and read horror novels.

Brad Sibley

Brad Sibley is an Infrastructure Technologist for Flint Hills Resources, LP, a Wichita, Kansas -based refining and chemicals company wholly owned by Koch Industries, Inc., also headquartered in Wichita. In his current role he is also responsible for participating in FHR IT security initiatives/projects and is a member of the team that supports the FHR storage area network. Prior to coming to FHR, Brad worked for 12 years in various IT positions for Conoco, Inc. He has worked in the IT field for 18+ years, 10 as a software developer/analyst and the past 8+ as a UNIX technologist, working primarily with Sun Solaris and HP-UX systems. Brad holds a B.S. in Mathematics/Computer Science from Oklahoma Christian University. In his spare time, he enjoys hunting/fishing, flower gardening, and dabbling in photography.

Contributing Authors

Ralph Durkee

Ralph has 23 years experience and has been an independent consultant since 1996. His specialty is Internet security and software development consulting, as well as web and e-mail hosting at http://rd1.net. Ralph holds the SANS GIAC "Security Essentials" (GSEC) and "Hacker Techniques, Exploits and Incident Handling" (GCIH) certifications, and is the Rochester, NY Local Mentor for the GSEC and GCIH.

Erik Kamerling

Erik Kamerling is an Information Security Analyst with Pragmeta Network Consulting, LLC. He is also the Lead Grader for the Global Information Assurance (GIAC) Security Essentials (GSEC) certification.

Steven Sipes

Steven is employed by Computer Sciences Corporation and holds the GSEC, GCIH and CISSP certifications. He is also on the GCIH advisory board.

Reviewers

Andreas Chatziantoniou, Antonio G. Sánchez Funes, Roland Grefer, Brian Hatch, Ian Hayes, Richard Hayler, Eric Hobbs, Betty Kelly, Tim Maletic, Daniel Mellen, Greg Owens, Ariya Parsamanesh, Felix Schallock, George Starcher, Rob Smith, Richard Wanner

Special thanks to:

Roland Grefer
Stephen Northcutt
Suzy Northcutt
Elle Vitt

---

* UNIX is a registered trademark of The Open Group in the United States and other countries.

Introduction

Our goal in writing the *OpenSSH Step-by-Step* is to empower you with the ability to proficiently use the OpenSSH toolset. After reading these step-by-step instructions, we believe you will be able to use OpenSSH to create secure, encrypted connections to remote servers and exchange data without the worry of a malicious attacker intercepting and reading your information in transit.

The OpenSSH suite of tools provides replacements for some of the common administrative tools used today such as telnet, FTP and the Berkeley r-commands (`rlogin`, `rcp` and `rsh`). These tools are considered insecure because they use clear-text connections over the network. This means they do not encrypt any of the transmitted network traffic, so anyone with sufficient privileges on any machine between your computer and the remote server to which you are connected could see the data from your connection, including your password. OpenSSH provides an encrypted channel between your computer and the remote server so if anyone were able to see your network traffic, they would not be able to tell what is occurring.

OpenSSH also provides strong authentication to remote servers. Programs like telnet, FTP or the Berkeley r-commands typically use passwords to authenticate. The problem with this approach is if anyone were to discover a user's password, they could log in and impersonate the user. OpenSSH can be configured to authenticate in a number of ways. First, it can validate the hosts involved through the exchange of host keys. Second, it also supports public key authentication in addition to password authentication. Public key authentication involves authentication using public/private key pairs. Through this method SSH assures that the only persons able to authenticate to a server are those that 1) hold a private key that matches a corresponding public key on the server, and 2) know the passphrase that unlocks the key. Since passphrases should be longer and more complicated than passwords, compromising the passphrase is much more unlikely.

While OpenSSH replaces programs like FTP, telnet, and the Berkeley r-commands with encrypted counterparts, it also provides the ability to create an encrypted channel for other programs. Using a feature called Port Forwarding, SSH can create an encrypted tunnel for any program using TCP-based communications from your computer to a remote server.

An example of this would be your email connection. You most likely use the POP3 or IMAP protocol to retrieve your email and SMTP to send your email. Each of these protocols is clear-text and anyone between your computer and your mail server can see your email and the password you use to get it. As long as you have the appropriate access on your mail server, you can use SSH and port forwarding to encrypt your connection to your mail server.

The X Windows System on UNIX-based machines also has a number of severe vulnerabilities and can be very cumbersome to use when a firewall is between the client and server machines. OpenSSH provides a feature called X11 Forwarding which will transparently forward any remote X session to your local desktop through an encrypted tunnel.

If the benefits of using OpenSSH are not clear to you now, they should be after you read this guide.

Foreword – Selling OpenSSH to Management

The era in which businesses could safely manage their computers and networks using clear-text protocols, weak authentication mechanisms, and unencrypted channels is over. As we all know, the Internet has undergone explosive growth since its inception. The exponentially increasing rate at which new nodes are being connected to this network has caused a dramatic increase in the number of security risks and vulnerabilities that typically parallel such growth. It is a commonly held belief that the need for strong encryption and authentication in the management of our computing assets and infrastructure now far outweighs the temptation to use ubiquitously deployed clear-text protocols and management tools.

There are many inherent dangers when sending information across a network without the protection of encryption and they all have the potential to negatively impact your business. The risks and vulnerabilities caused by clear text protocol usage are all based on the compromise of the confidentiality, integrity, or availability of your company's computing assets. The actual compromise of your clear-text protocol management practices may arise from common attacks such as the passive monitoring of your network for unencrypted usernames and passwords, proxy type man-in-the-middle attacks, and ARP spoofing or poisoning attacks. Such security compromises result in high-level management issues such as public relations problems, loss of customer confidence, and compromise or theft of intellectual property or sensitive/classified information, all of which spell real loss of revenue for your company and its investors or serious breach of security and violation of protocol for governmental organizations.

According to the 2001 Information Security Magazine Industry Survey, a compilation of data collected from 2545 Information Security Practitioners, the percentage of respondents who experienced an externally originating security breach related to protocol weakness was 23 percent for 2001[1]. Couple this with the interesting findings by the Honeynet project on the average cost per security breach and we can begin to get a feel for the financial gravity of this situation. Using the Incident Cost Analysis Modeling Project (I-CAMP) model[2], the Honeynet project derived an average cost of $2,000 per security breach[3], involving a comprehensive investigation and cleanup after a full-blown compromise. A clear-text protocol attack run against your unprotected network will usually result in a significant gain in privilege level that would generate comparable recovery costs for your organization. If we take an objective look at correlated statistics of this sort, it becomes plainly evident that securing our systems against easily corrected security vulnerabilities is simply good business. Similarly, risk minimization efforts of this nature result in great benefit to government agencies and other entities of the public sector.

It is an unfortunate truth that modern operating systems are still being deployed today with clear-text protocols and vulnerable services enabled. Connecting such systems to the public network without taking the necessary steps to update them with appropriate patches and upgrades and to disable listening clear-text protocol applications and replace them with encrypted equivalents will have adverse effects, frequently causing downtime, loss of functionality, and lost revenue for the enterprise.

---

[1] http://www.infosecuritymag.com/articles/october01/images/survey.pdf figure 12 "Outsider/External Breaches"
[2] http://www.usenix.org/publications/login/1999-6/icamp.html
[3] http://project.honeynet.org/challenge/results/

The SANS/FBI Top 20 List of Critical Internet Security Vulnerabilities – The Experts Consensus[4], produced in conjunction with the National Infrastructure Protection Center, outlines the 20 most commonly exploited security vulnerabilities that attackers target on a daily basis. At the time of this writing, the updated SANS/FBI Top 20 List contains at least 3 commonly exploited UNIX vulnerabilities (U5 File Transfer Protocol, U6 R-Services – Trust Relationships, and U10 General UNIX Authentication – Accounts with No Passwords or Weak Passwords) that can be effectively remediated by replacing the vulnerable service or countering the vulnerability with a properly configured OpenSSH installation.

In order to demonstrate whether a threat exists to your enterprise in this regard, consider these two DShield[5] graphs demonstrating attacker activity focused on finding listening telnet (port 23) services and ftp (port 21) services over a 40-day period ending 02-13-2003. Note: both services are clear-text/unencrypted applications and are obviously being targeted by attackers.

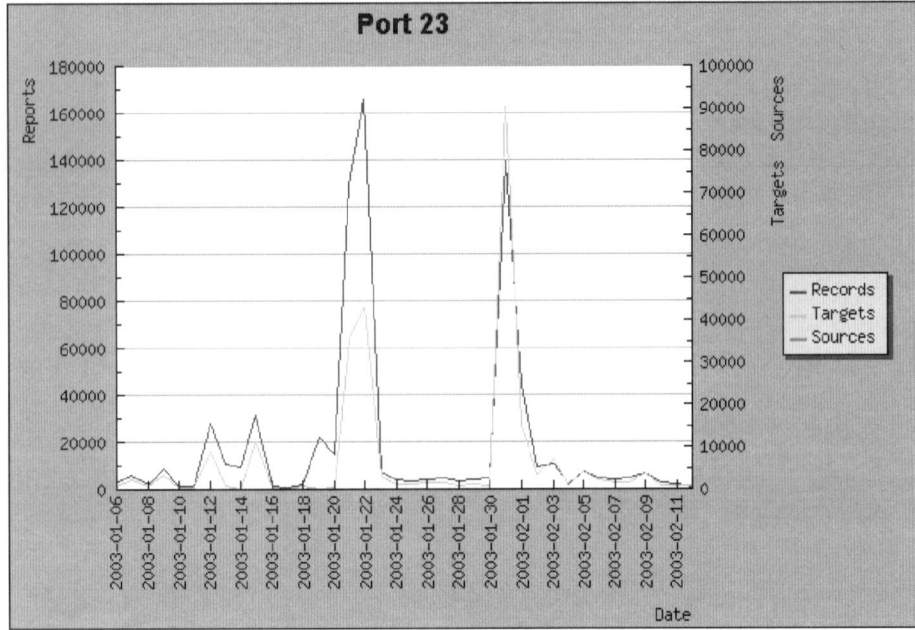

---

[4] SANS/FBI Top 20 List: Twenty Most Critical Internet Security Vulnerabilities – The Experts Consensus http://www.sans.org/top20
[5] DShield – http://www.dshield.org

Graph 2. Targeted FTPD

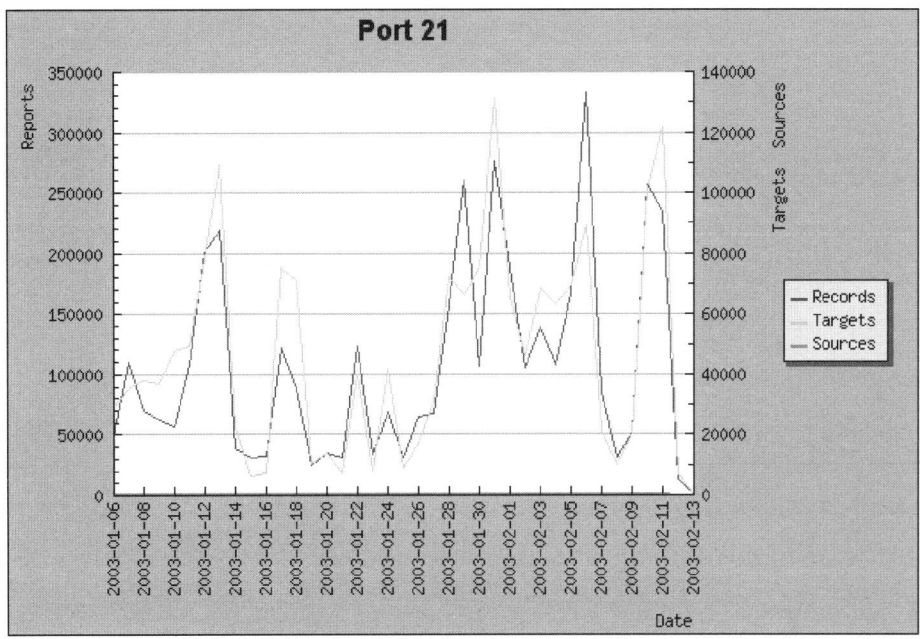

The use of firewalls and related access control devices helps greatly in defending your internal computing resources from Internet-borne attacks. Technologies such as Network Address Translation (NAT), Port Address Translation (PAT), application content and URL filtering, and various other Ingress and Egress network traffic control techniques comprise some of the most valuable network security investments your business can make. Yet, clear-text protocol use is still prevalent in most enterprises (e.g. FTP, TELNET, POP), even though this can be rectified at very little cost with tools like OpenSSH[6] and equivalent or complementary encryption programs like OpenSSL.[7]

OpenSSH is free of charge for personal as well as commercial use, and is released under a BSD license by the OpenBSD Project.[8] With the existence of free, industry proven encryption technologies such as OpenSSH, companies no longer have an excuse for using clear-text protocols for managing their critical infrastructure.

[6] OpenSSH – http://www.openssh.com
[7] OpenSSL – http://www.openssl.org
[8] OpenBSD – http://www.openbsd.org

There are a number of standard methods by which we can estimate the potential risk and asset loss involved by not implementing encryption -- Delphi/Modified Delphi Techniques[9] and the standard Information Security tenet of Risk = Threat x Vulnerability x Cost or Asset Worth are two such methods.[10] Mitigating risk should be one of the primary objectives of any information security initiative in your company, and technologies such as OpenSSH play a highly important role in such alleviation efforts.

Posing a few questions also provides support for these equations, methods, and associated conclusions.

1. How much is it worth to your enterprise if human resources data is intercepted in transit and your company's salary data becomes public information?

2. How do you quantify the loss associated with the premature release of information regarding your enterprise financial performance on the eve of Initial Public Offering? What is the cost before and after a loss, if it could have been mitigated with a free product?

3. Can you assign a dollar figure to the potential loss of your organization's intellectual property or sensitive/classified data that has been transmitted using clear-text protocols?

4. If you are in the healthcare industry, is it possible to quantify the potential loss arising from compromised patient medical data, particularly since you have been charged with guaranteeing the security and privacy of such data according to HIPAA regulations?

5. If you are a government agency, keep in mind that numerous organizations such as The Office of Management and Budget (OMB), The National Institute of Standards and Technology (NIST), and various initiatives such as the Government Information Security Reform Act (GISRA) and Presidential Decision Directives (PDD) require that you protect your systems and data.

These types of questions are vitally important to ask when you are attempting to gauge the business validity of clear-text protocol replacement initiatives. By developing effective vulnerability assessment equations for your enterprise and asking the right questions about asset worth, you will invariably arrive at the conclusion that data encryption for your business is a required security measure.

Regardless of the outcome of your own vulnerability and risk assessment, there will always be inherent and significant vulnerabilities in the transmission of data in unencrypted form. The almost universal distribution of vulnerable clear-text programs, protocols, networked systems, and weak authentication mechanisms should be considered a significant danger to the business community at large. As long as free, industry proven tools exist that can aid your enterprise in minimizing its risk and eliminating threats it is exposed to on a daily basis, the question we should really be asking ourselves is "Can we afford NOT to implement OpenSSH as a standard defensive measure within our enterprise?"

---

[9] Delphi/Modified Delphi Techniques – *Information Warfare and Security*, Denning Dorothy page 385-388
[10] Risk = Theat x Vulnerability x Cost or Asset Worth http://www.giac.org/practical/gsec/David_Beck_GSEC.pdf

Section I - Obtaining, Compiling And Installing OpenSSH

Problem: The common UNIX remote access protocols – telnet, FTP and the Berkeley r-commands -- are unencrypted. Account and password information can easily be sniffed by unauthorized intruders and others who have been granted access to the same network. OpenSSH can be used to encrypt all remote sessions, thereby eliminating this vulnerability.

Step 1.1 Install OpenSSH to Replace the Remote Access Protocols with Encrypted Versions

OpenSSH is free and runs on virtually all of the different UNIX and Linux variants. Zlib, a compression library and OpenSSL, the secure sockets layer software, are required by OpenSSH, so you need to install them first. Also highly recommended is a suitable random number generator.

> *Note: The examples and instructions in this section demonstrate installation and configuration of Zlib, ANDIrand, PRNGD, OpenSSL, and OpenSSH on Solaris 8. Depending on the version of UNIX/Linux you are running, there will be some slight variation in specifics.*

> **Tech Tip**
> In the installation/configuration sections which follow, it is highly recommended and in keeping with best security practices that **1)** the integrity of downloads is verified with any mechanisms made available to you, such as checksums and/or cryptographic signatures, and **2)** all steps be performed using non-root accounts, except for those which require root permissions.

Action 1.1.1 Download and install the GNU C compiler

Since all the software to install is in source code format and will have to be compiled, you need to make sure that you have a C compiler installed. If not, download and install the GNU C compiler.

- Point your web browser to <http://gcc.gnu.org/install/binaries.html>.
- Click on the **Solaris 2 – Sunfreeware** link.
- Click on **FTP/Mirror Sites** on the left-hand column, and then choose one of the mirror sites (generally you will get better download performance from a mirror site).
- Click on **Sparc/Solaris 8** on the right-hand column to see the list of software available for Solaris 8; scroll down and click on the latest release of gcc (3.2 as of this writing)
- Usually the latest gcc package will appear at the top of the page, e.g. **gcc-3.2-sol8-sparc-local.gz**. Download this package into /usr/local.
- Uncompress the .gz file, as shown below:
  ```
  $  cd /usr/local
  $  gunzip ./gcc-3.2-sol8-sparc-local.gz
  ```
- Use `pkgadd` to install the gcc binaries, as shown below:
  ```
  $ su
  Password: ********
  # pkgadd -d ./gcc-3.2-sol8-sparc-local
  ```

This will install a new Solaris package named SMCgcc. The gcc binary will be placed in /usr/local/bin. Use pkginfo to verify the installation, as shown below:

```
# pkginfo -l SMCgcc
    PKGINST:  SMCgcc
       NAME:  gcc
   CATEGORY:  application
       ARCH:  sparc
    VERSION:  3.2
    BASEDIR:  /usr/local
     VENDOR:  Free Software Foundation
     PSTAMP:  Steve Christensen
   INSTDATE:  Nov 14 2002 16:52
      EMAIL:  steve@smc.vnet.net
     STATUS:  completely installed
      FILES:      1776 installed pathnames
                     4 linked files
                   136 directories
                    43 executables
                548584 blocks used (approx)
```

Action 1.1.2 Download, compile and install Zlib compression library

- Point your web browser to <u>http://www.gzip.org/zlib</u>.

- Download the latest version of the ".gz" format of Zlib (1.1.4 as of this writing) into /usr/local.

- Use gunzip and tar to extract the source code, as shown below:
  ```
  $ cd /usr/local
  $ gunzip ./zlib-1.1.4.tar.gz
  $ tar xvf ./zlib-1.1.4.tar
  ```

This will create a source-code directory structure such as /usr/local/zlib-1.1.4.

- Review the README and Makefile files.

- Configure, make and compile, as shown below:
  ```
  $ cd /usr/local/zlib-1.1.4
  $ ./configure
  $ make test
  $ su
  Password: ********
  # make install
  ```

Action 1.1.3 Download, compile and install a random number generator

Some UNIX implementations, such as Solaris 8, do not provide a random number generator (e.g. /dev/random) out of the box. OpenSSL will automatically provide a random number generator if one is not found on the system, but it is highly recommended to use a higher quality random number generator, such as ANDIrand, PRNGD or EGD. Instructions are provided below for both ANDIrand and PRNGD.

ANDIrand

ANDIrand is a simple package install (as opposed to a source-code compile) and creates the /dev/random and /dev/urandom devices at install time, from which SSL, one of the prerequisites to OpenSSH, obtains its random data.

- Point your web browser to http://www.cosy.sbg.ac.at/~andi/SUNrand/.
- Download the latest version of the package format (0.7 of this writing) into /usr/local.
- Use pkgadd to install the ANDIrand binaries as user root, as shown below:
  ```
  # cd /usr/local
  # pkgadd -d ./ANDIrand-0.7-5.8-sparc-1.pkg
  ```

> **Note:** You will be prompted as to whether to continue to install the package with root privileges – enter "Y" to continue

This will install a new Solaris package named ANDIrand and will also create the /dev/random and /dev/urandom files on your system. Use `pkginfo -l` to see the details for the install:

```
# pkginfo -l ANDIrand
   PKGINST:  ANDIrand
      NAME:  random-0.7
  CATEGORY:  system
      ARCH:  sparc
   VERSION:  0.7
    VENDOR:  Andreas Maier
      DESC:  random number generator
    PSTAMP:  200111201124
  INSTDATE:  Nov 18 2002 14:28
   HOTLINE:  http://www.cosy.sbg.ac.at/~andi/
     EMAIL:  andi@cosy.sbg.ac.at
    STATUS:  completely installed
     FILES:       13 installed pathnames
                   8 shared pathnames
                   2 linked files
                   7 directories
                   2 executables
                  26 blocks used (approx)
```

PRNGD
PRNGD is a source-code compile, which creates a prngd executable to be run as a daemon on the UNIX system.

- Point your web browser to <http://www.aet.tu-cottbus.de/personen/jaenicke/postfix_tls/prngd.html>
- Click on the **prngd 0.9.27** link in the Download section to download the latest version of the prngd source-code (0.9.27 of this writing) into /usr/local
- Use gunzip and tar to extract the source code, as shown below:
  ```
  $ cd /usr/local
  $ gunzip ./prngd-0.9.27.tar.gz
  $ tar xvf ./prngd-0.9.27.tar
  $ cd ./prngd-0.9.27
  ```

This will create a source-code directory structure such as /usr/local/prngd-0.9.27.

- Review the 00README file for compile and install instructions
- Use your favorite editor to edit the "Makefile" file and make the following 2 changes:
    1. Scroll down to the section corresponding to your particular OS and uncomment the lines in that section.
    2. Scroll down to the section beginning with "# Move default locations" and select a default location for storing the prngd-seed and prngd.conf files. (if you don't specify a "new" default location, the default is /usr/local/etc/prngd).
- Become root
  ```
  $ su
  Password:    *********
  #
  ```
- After saving changes to the Makefile, run make to compile the prngd source code:
  ```
  # make
  ```
- Copy the prngd executable to /usr/local/sbin
  ```
  # cp -p ./prngd /usr/local/sbin
  ```
- Copy a default prngd.conf file. There are sample prngd.conf files for numerous OS' under the contrib subdirectory. The location of the prngd.conf file should be consistent with what you specified earlier when you edited the Makefile. In the following example, a sample Solaris prngd.conf file is copied to the default location of /usr/local/etc/prngd:
  ```
  # pwd
  /usr/local/prngd-0.9.27
  # cd contrib
  # ls
  AIX-3.2         IRIX-65         OSF1            SCO3            SunOS-4
  AIX-4.3         Linux-2         OSR5            Solaris-2.6     Tru64
  ATT-NCR         MacOSX-10       OpenUNIX-8      Solaris-7       Ultrix-4.5
  HPUX            NeXTStep-3.3    ReliantUNIX     Solaris-8       Unixware-7
  # cd Solaris-7
  # ls
  prngd.conf.solaris-7
  # cp ./prngd.conf.solaris-7 /usr/local/etc/prngd/prngd.conf
  ```

> *Note: The Solaris-8 directory simply has instructions to use the conf file from the Solaris-7 directory.*

- Use the following command to generate an initial "seed" for PRNGD:
  ```
  # cat /var/adm/messages /var/log/syslog > /usr/local/etc/prngd/prngd-seed
  ```
- Start PRNGD:
  ```
  # /usr/local/sbin/prngd /var/run/egd-pool
  ```

Since PRNGD is a daemon, you'll want to be sure to create a startup script and place it in the appropriate OS startup directory so the system will automatically start PRNGD on system startup. There are sample startup scripts for most OS' in the "contrib" sub-directory:

```
# pwd
/usr/local/prngd-0.9.27
# cd contrib
# ls
AIX-3.2       IRIX-65        OSF1          SCO3          SunOS-4
AIX-4.3       Linux-2        OSR5          Solaris-2.6   Tru64
ATT-NCR       MacOSX-10      OpenUNIX-8    Solaris-7     Ultrix-4.5
HPUX          NeXTStep-3.3   ReliantUNIX   Solaris-8     Unixware-7
```

Action 1.1.4 Download, compile and install OpenSSL

- Point your web browser to http://www.openssl.org/source/
- Download the latest version of the source code (0.9.7b as of this writing) into /usr/local
- Use `gunzip` and `tar` to extract the source code, as shown below:
  ```
  $ cd /usr/local
  $ gunzip ./openssl-0.9.7b.tar.gz
  $ tar xvf ./openssl-0.9.7b.tar
  $ cd openssl-0.9.7b
  ```

This will create the source-code directory structure, such as /usr/local/openssl-0.9.7b

- Review the README and INSTALL files
- Configure, make and compile, as shown below:
  ```
  $ ./config
  $ make              (go for coffee, this takes awhile)
  $ make test
  $ su
  Password: ********
  # make install
  ```

Action 1.1.5 Download, compile and install OpenSSH

- Point your web browser to <u>http://www.openssh.com/portable.html</u>
- Download the latest version of the source code (3.6.1p2 as of this writing) into `/usr/local`
- Use `gunzip` and `tar` to extract the source code, as shown below:
  ```
  $ cd /usr/local
  $ gunzip ./openssh-3.6.1p2.tar.gz
  $ tar xvf ./openssh-3.6.1p2.tar
  ```

This will create a source-code directory structure such as `/usr/local/openssh-3.6.1p2`.

- Review the README and INSTALL files.
- Issue the following commands to configure, make and compile OpenSSH. The default options, such as where the binaries will be installed, can be changed when the configure script is run. The options can be displayed by running `./configure -help`.
  ```
  $ cd /usr/local/openssh-3.6.1p2
  $ ./configure
  $ make
  $ su
  Password: ********
  ```
- The OpenSSH software requires that we have an `sshd` UNIX account defined before it will start the "sshd" daemon. If we do not do this before we run `make install`, we will see the message "Privilege separation user sshd does not exist" at the end of the `make install` output.

Since we do not want anyone logging in directly to this account, we should make it a non-interactive account. The following command creates the `sshd` user with a user id of 1100 and an invalid shell that prevents anyone from logging in directly:
```
# useradd -c "sshd owner" -d /var/empty \
-u 1100 -s /bin/false sshd
```

If the home directory for this account, `/var/empty`, does not exist, it should be created as follows:
```
# mkdir /var/empty
# chmod 555 /var/empty
```

As an extra measure of securing this account, issue the following command to lock it:
```
# passwd -l sshd
```

- Once the "sshd" user is created, OpenSSH can be installed as shown below.
  ```
  # make install
  ```

At the end of the make install output, you should see messages similar to the following:

```
Generating public/private rsa1 key pair.
Your identification has been saved in /usr/local/etc/ssh_host_key.
Your public key has been saved in /usr/local/etc/ssh_host_key.pub.
The key fingerprint is:
71:9f:97:e7:23:53:1e:38:84:f2:91:ff:bc:6e:4a:59 root@client.example.com
Generating public/private dsa key pair.
Your identification has been saved in /usr/local/etc/ssh_host_dsa_key.
Your public key has been saved in /usr/local/etc/ssh_host_dsa_key.pub.
The key fingerprint is:
24:95:93:f2:9f:c8:68:37:08:32:f8:12:95:63:26:3a root@client.example.com
Generating public/private rsa key pair.
Your identification has been saved in /usr/local/etc/ssh_host_rsa_key.
Your public key has been saved in /usr/local/etc/ssh_host_rsa_key.pub.
The key fingerprint is:
45:a1:35:51:06:2d:0d:0f:1a:0c:a4:ab:41:05:cd:70 root@client.example.com
/usr/local/sbin/sshd -t -f /usr/local/etc/sshd_config
```

Congratulations – you have successfully installed the OpenSSH software – both client-side and server-side. If the machine on which you installed will function as an OpenSSH client only (i.e., will initiate connections to remote systems, but not accept remote connections), then we're ready to test and verify that the installation is correct. If the machine will be an OpenSSH client and server (will accept remote connections) or an OpenSSH server only, there are a few more steps to perform.

Action 1.1.6 Configure the sshd_config configuration file

Now that the OpenSSH software is installed, we need to make sure the server configuration is set up correctly. The configuration file for the SSH daemon is usually located in /etc/ssh and is called sshd_config. You can leave most of the settings alone as the defaults should work for most installations. However, the following should be verified to make sure they are set correctly.

Appendix A of this book contains a sample sshd_config file with comments pertaining to each option. This sample configuration file should work for most, if not all, current versions of OpenSSH.

> *Note: In the OpenSSH configuration files, the absence of an option means OpenSSH will use the default settings for that option as specified in the man page for sshd.*

- **Protocol** – The **Protocol** option sets which SSH protocol version to use. By default, SSHv1 and SSHv2 are permitted. Protocol version 1 has a number of vulnerabilities and its use is discouraged. More information on protocol version 1's problems can be found at
  http://www.openssh.com/security.html

  OpenSSH should be set to only allow SSHv2 connections. To do this, uncomment the line "Protocol" in sshd_config and place only a "2" after it, as shown below:
  ```
  Protocol 2
  ```

- **PermitRootLogin** – is a setting which specifies whether or not root is allowed to log in remotely to the server. By default, OpenSSH allows this. Allowing root to log in remotely is typically discouraged since it provides one more avenue for an attacker to target and if root is compromised, an entire system is compromised. To disable the ability to remotely log in as root, change the "PermitRootLogin" as shown below:
  ```
  PermitRootLogin no
  ```

- **PubkeyAuthentication** – specifies whether or not SSHv2 public key authentication is allowed to be used. By default, this is set to "yes". If you plan on using public key authentication, you should verify that this option is still set to "yes". You can manually allow public key authentication by setting the option as shown below:
  ```
  PubkeyAuthentication yes
  ```

- **X11Forwarding** – specifies whether or not the OpenSSH daemon will allow connecting clients to use **X11 Forwarding**. **X11 Forwarding** is explained in detail in Step 6.3.

  By default, this is not allowed. If you wish to allow incoming clients the ability to use the **X11 Forwarding** feature of OpenSSH, set the **X11Forwarding** option as shown below:
  ```
  X11Forwarding yes
  ```

- Banner – The Banner option specifies a text file that will be displayed whenever anyone connects to the server with an SSH client. This may be required for legal purposes. The Banner option can be set as shown below:
  ```
  banner /etc/issue
  ```

Action 1.1.7 Configure auto-start of sshd daemon (for OpenSSH server)

The OpenSSH server daemon, sshd, must be started before OpenSSH clients will be allowed to connect.

You can simply launch the sshd daemon as root and place it in the background as follows:
```
# /usr/local/sbin/sshd &
```

You should also place this command in a startup script so that it launches each time the system is booted. For example, on Solaris 8 we could use an editor to insert and save the above command in the file /etc/init.d/sshd_start, then issue the following commands:
```
# ln /etc/init.d/sshd_start /etc/rc3.d/S95sshd
```

Now each time the system is booted, the sshd daemon will start automatically as user "sshd".

Problem: Many times administrators will find themselves on a Windows machine with no way to access a remote server securely since Microsoft does not yet package an SSH client.

Step 1.2 Install SSH Windows Clients to Access Remote Machines Securely

There are a number of excellent tools available that provide SSH client connectivity from a Windows platform. A list of these tools is available at `http://www.openssh.com/windows.html`.

> *Note: It is possible to use Cygwin, a UNIX environment for Windows, to compile OpenSSH and run an OpenSSH server daemon. However, installing and configuring Cygwin is beyond the scope of this book and will not be discussed. Cygwin can be found at http://sources.redhat.com/cygwin/.*

Action 1.2.1 Download and install PuTTY for Windows

PuTTY is an open source Windows SSH and telnet client, distributed under the MIT license and maintained by Simon Tatham. The package contains all of the necessary components required to connect to a machine running the OpenSSH server and runs on all versions of Windows, starting at Windows 95.

PuTTY contains a number of components that are described below.

1. PuTTY – This is an SSH and telnet client that can be run through the Windows graphical user interface (GUI) or from the command line. It supports SSHv1 and SSHv2.
2. PSCP – This is a command line scp client.
3. PSFTP – This is a command line sftp client. PSFTP will only work on SSH servers that support SSHv2 since the SFTP protocol is supported only there.
4. PuTTYtel – This is a telnet only client.
5. Plink – This is a command line interface to PuTTY that can be used within scripts to create secure connections to SSH servers.
6. Pageant – This is an SSH authentication agent that will keep your private keys unencrypted in memory so you do not have to enter your passphrase every time you authenticate to a server.
7. PuTTYgen – This is a key generation utility that will create RSA1, RSA and DSA public/private key pairs.

Each of these components can function separately, although the purpose of some is to complement what the others do. For example, Pageant is used to provide automatic authentication for PuTTY, PSCP and PSFTP.

To install PuTTY onto your Windows machine, the following steps need to be taken:

- Point your web browser to `http://www.chiark.greenend.org.uk/~sgtatham/putty/download.html`
- The easiest way to download and install PuTTY is to scroll down to the section entitled **A Windows-style installer (x86) for everything except PuTTYtel** and click on the link provided. This will allow you to download all of the PuTTY components except the telnet-only client.
- The first box to pop up is the **File Download** dialog box asking if you want to Open, Save or Cancel this operation. A good practice when downloading software is to save it to your hard drive. If you have a virus scanner installed, this will allow you to easily determine if the software is infected with a virus, and has the benefit of preserving the software locally if a reinstall should become necessary. In general, it is not advisable to execute a program directly from the download site.

- Once the installer has downloaded, double-click on the file to start the installation.
- The first box will ask if you want to install PuTTY. Click **Yes**.
- The next box is the initial welcome screen asking you to close down any other applications. While it may not be necessary to close down every other program you have open at this time, it is probably a good idea to prevent any problems. Once you have closed down any open programs, click **Next**.
- The next box asks for the directory where you would like PuTTY installed. Choose the directory into which you would like it installed and click **Next**. This installation directory should be noted as it will be needed when setting the Windows path in an upcoming step.
- The next box asks you in what Start Menu folder to place PuTTY's shortcuts. Choose an existing folder or create your own and click **Next**.
- Next, you will be asked whether or not you would like to create:
    A **Start Menu** group — this will create a folder within the Start Menu for easy access
    A **desktop icon** for PuTTY — convenient desktop access
    Associate .PPK files with Pageant — this associates files with the PPK extension with Pageant files. PPK files are where PuTTY stores your private keys.

    Choose which items you want the installation to complete and click **Next**. If you are not sure which items should be created, leave them all checked and click **Next**.
- Finally, you are shown the choices you have made. If all are correct, click **Install**, else click **Back** and redo any choices.
- After the install is finished, you will see a window that confirms that the install was successful. Click the **Finish** button to complete the install. PuTTY is now installed and ready for use.

Since most of PuTTY's components are command line based, it may be helpful to have them in your Windows PATH so you can execute them while at the Windows command prompt. This is done differently in each version of Windows.

For Windows XP:

- Go to the **Start Menu** and right click on the **My Computer** icon. From there, select **Properties**.
- In the next box click on the **Advanced** tab and then click on the button marked **Environment Variables**.
- In the next box you will see a window marked **System Variables**. This box contains a number of environment variables Windows uses. Scroll through the list and look for the "Path" variable — highlight it and then click **Edit**.
- The next box will show you a Variable name and a Variable value. Click *once* on the Variable value. *DO NOT ERASE* this value -- simply go to the far right and add the following:
    `;C:\program files\putty`
    where `c:\program files\putty` is the default directory in which the PuTTY programs are installed.
- Click **OK** until you are back at the desktop.

To check your PATH go back to the **Start Menu** and click on **Run**. Type in `cmd` and Click **OK**.

A Windows command prompt should appear. Type "PuTTY". If your path has been set correctly, the PuTTY configuration box should appear.

To change the PATH from a Windows command prompt: the path can be set as shown below:
```
C:\> set PATH=%PATH%;c:\program files\putty
```

where `c:\program files\putty` is the default directory the PuTTY programs are installed. If typed on the Windows command prompt in this manner, the command must be repeated for each new command window opened; it will not be saved for future command windows.

Action 1.2.2 Download and install WinSCP - a graphical SSH file transfer tool
The file transfer tools that come with PuTTY are command line based, which can make it difficult in a Windows environment to quickly and easily transfer files. However, there are a number of graphical SSH file transfer tools referenced at http://www.openssh.com/windows.html. One such tool is WinSCP.

WinSCP is a freeware scp-like client maintained by Martin Prikryl and is located at http://winscp.vse.cz/eng. It provides a Windows Explorer- or Norton Commander-type drag-and-drop interface for transferring files securely and easily from one computer to the next, using SSH.

- Point your web browser to http://winscp.vse.cz/eng/download.php.
- At the time of this writing, the latest version of WinSCP available for download is WinSCP 2.3.0. To download WinSCP 2.3.0, click on the link for **WinSCP 2.3.0 installation package**.
- The first box to pop up is a **File Download** dialog box asking if you want to Open, Save or Cancel this operation. A good practice when downloading software is to save it to your hard drive. If you have a virus scanner installed, this will allow you to easily determine if the software is infected with a virus, and has the benefit of preserving the software locally if a reinstall should become necessary. In general it is not advisable to execute a program directly from the download site.
- Once the WinSCP install program has completed downloading, double-click on it to start the installation.
- After double-clicking on the install program, the **WinSCP Setup Wizard** appears. The first box is the initial Welcome Screen asking you to close down any other applications. While it may not be necessary to close down every other program you have open at this time, it is probably a good idea to prevent any problems. Once you have closed down any open programs, click **Next**.
- The next box is the **License Agreement**. Read through the license agreement and if you agree to it, click the radio button next to "I accept the agreement" and click **Next**.
- The next box is the directory where you would like WinSCP installed. Choose the directory into which you would like WinSCP installed and click **Next**.
- The next window asks you to select the components to install. The components you are given the option to install are:

    WinSCP application – This is the main application. You want to install this.
    PuTTYgen – This is the key generator from PuTTY that WinSCP uses. Even if you already have PuTTYgen installed, you probably want to install this as it may be a different version than what you already have installed.
    Pageant – This is the SSH authentication agent from PuTTY that WinSCP uses. Like PuTTYgen, you probably want to install this as well.

    Once you have selected the components to install, click **Next**.

- The next box asks you in what Start Menu folder to place WinSCP's shortcuts. Choose an existing folder or create your own and click **Next**.
- The next prompt will ask you to **Select Additional Tasks**. You are given a choice of the following tasks you would like the setup program to perform:

    Create a desktop icon — This will create an icon for WinSCP on the desktop.
    Create a Quick Launch icon — This will put an icon in your quick launch menu along your Taskbar.
    Add upload shortcut to Explorer's 'Send to' context menu — This will allow you to right click on a file within Windows Explorer and begin an upload.
    Choose the tasks you prefer and then click **Next**.

- The next screen asks you to select your initial user settings.

    User Interface style — You are given the choice between a Norton Commander or Windows Explorer-style interface. The Norton Commander style will show the local and remote system in two windows side-by-side while the Window Explorer style will display the remote folder as a window by itself.
    Show advanced login options — This will show the advanced options you are able to set when the WinSCP initial login screen appears.

    Choose the interface settings you prefer and click **Next**.

- Finally, you are shown the choices you have made. If these are correct, click **Install**, else click **Back** and redo any choices.
- After the install is finished, you will see a window that confirms the install was successful. Click the **Finish** button to complete the install. WinSCP is now installed and ready for use.

If WinSCP is installed correctly, the WinSCP login screen shown below should display.

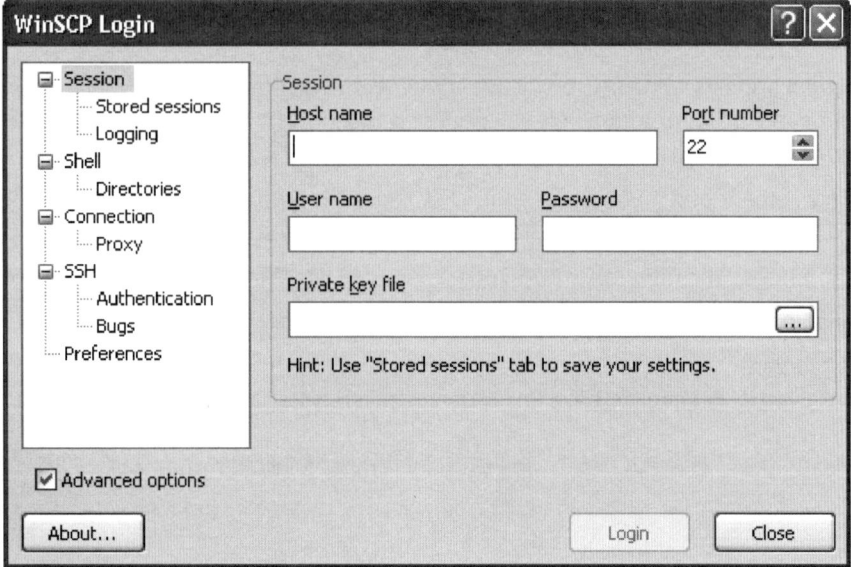

Section 2 - How To Use OpenSSH Clients For UNIX-To-UNIX Connectivity

Problem: Now that the OpenSSH software is installed, we need to learn how to utilize it for invoking remote interactive connections and transferring files. We also need some way to verify that our connections are truly encrypted.

Step 2.1 Use the OpenSSH Tool Suite to Replace Clear-Text Programs

Action 2.1.1 - Use OpenSSH as a replacement for telnet/rsh/rlogin
The `ssh` command is used to make secure, remote, interactive connections. This command can be used as the replacement for the unencrypted `telnet`, `rsh` and `rlogin` programs.

The format of the ssh command is as follows:
ssh [**-l** *login_name*] *hostname* | *user@hostname* [*command*]

where:
> *login_name* = the account you are attempting to access on the remote system
> *hostname* = the remote system
> *user@hostname* = this is just an alternate format for combining account and remote system info
> *command* = the command on the remote host you are wanting to run; if you want an interactive shell, you would leave this blank

The following is an example where the local system is trying to connect to remote system `server.example.com` with account `sshuser` to run the `ls -l` command:

```
$ ssh -l sshuser server.example.com ls -l
The authenticity of host 'server.example.com (172.16.121.6)' can't be established.
RSA key fingerprint is a4:f0:02:eb:11:84:70:c2:c3:24:18:61:89:49:ac:4b.
Are you sure you want to continue connecting (yes/no)? yes
Warning: Permanently added server.example.com,172.16.121.6' (RSA) to the list of known hosts

total 3188
-rw-r--r--  1   sshuser    admin            0 Feb 24  14:31  a
drwxr-xr-x 10   sshuser    admin          512 Dec 19  10:48  etc
drwx------  2   root       other          512 Jun 26   2000  nsmail
-rw-r--r--  1   sshuser    admin      1620193 May 15   2002  openssh31.zip
$
```

The first several lines of output are normal for the first time you connect to a particular system running an sshd daemon – after the first successful connection, you should not see these messages. However, prior to accepting this fingerprint and storing it in the list of known hosts, you will have to verify through a secure means that this is the correct fingerprint for the system to which you are attempting to connect.

In order to do this, somebody on the target machine will have to execute
```
$ ssh-keygen -l -f file
```

where `file` is the name of the host's public SSH key, such as `/etc/ssh/ssh_host_key.pub`. The result will look similar to the following and should match the key fingerprint previously given:
```
a4:f0:02:eb:11:84:70:c2:c3:24:18:61:89:49:ac:4b
```

Keep in mind that the fingerprint *must* be transmitted in a secure way (i.e. by a phone call to the administrator of the remote system), since SSH relies on these keys and the fingerprint is the simple proof for a valid key. For obvious reasons, SSH does not provide a way to fetch such fingerprints remotely from an SSH server.

Here is the second attempt using the same command:
```
$ ssh -l sshuser server.example.com ls
sshuser@server.example.com's password:
nsmail
openssh31.zip
$
```

If you wish to connect to the remote system and receive a shell (as opposed to running a command and then exiting), then omit the optional "command string". For example:
```
$ ssh -l sshuser server.example.com
sshuser@server.example.com's password:
Last login: Fri Nov 15 16:12:22 2002 from KII-1QZ7611
Sun Microsystems Inc.   SunOS 5.8       Generic February 2000
$
```

You can now proceed just as if you had connected via "telnet" and nothing should appear different to you. The only difference is that all the communication between the local and remote systems are now encrypted.

Action 2.1.2 - Use the sftp command as a replacement for FTP to exchange files with a remote system

The sftp command is used to perform file transfers to/from remote connections. This command can be used as the replacement for the unencrypted FTP program. This document assumes that you are familiar with FTP; sftp is very similar in that an initial command is issued to connect to an sftp server and if the authentication is successful, the client is placed into sftp interactive mode.

Although there are many options, the basic format of the sftp command is as follows:
sftp [*user@*]*hostname*

where:
    user = the account you are attempting to access on the remote system – if not specified, the current account name is assumed.
    hostname = the remote system

The following is an example where the local system connects via sftp to remote system server.example.com with account sshuser, then transfers a file from the remote /tmp filesystem:

```
$ sftp server.example.com
Connecting to server.example.com...
sshuser@server.example.com's password: ********
sftp> cd /tmp
sftp> ls
.
..
.X11-pipe
.X11-unix
.pcmcia
.removable
.s.PGSQL.5432
dtdbcache_172.16.124
dtdbcache_KII-1QZ7611:0
openssh-3.4p1
openssh-3.4p1.tar
openssl-0.9.6g
openssl-0.9.6g.tar
perl-5.8.0-sol8-sparc-local
ps_data
snoop.txt
sftp> lcd /tmp
sftp> get snoop.txt
Fetching /tmp/snoop.txt to snoop.txt
sftp> bye
$
```

If this sftp attempt is the first SSH connection attempted to the remote system, you will also receive an authenticity warning and a prompt similar to the following:

```
The authenticity of host 'server.example.com (172.16.121.6)' can't be established.
RSA key fingerprint is a4:f0:02:eb:11:84:70:c2:c3:24:18:61:89:49:ac:4b.
Are you sure you want to continue connecting (yes/no)? yes
```

> *Note: Once you enter "yes" to the prompt, the host will be added to the SSH "known hosts" file and you shouldn't be prompted with this information for subsequent attempts:*

```
Warning: Permanently added 'server.example.com,172.16.121.6' (RSA) to the list of known hosts
```

> **Note:** It is strongly recommended that the host key be verified the first time it is used to prevent potential risk of man-in-the-middle attacks. See Action 2.1.1 for instructions to verify the host's fingerprint.

You can also specify the user name as part of the sftp connection command, as shown below:

```
$ sftp sshuser@server.example.com
Connecting to server.example.com...
sshuser@server.example.com's password:   *********
sftp>
```

There are many command line options to sftp, too numerous to cover in this document. As always, use the man command to get the details, as shown below:

```
$ man sftp
Reformatting page.   Please Wait... done

User Commands                                                     SFTP(1)

NAME
     sftp - Secure file transfer program

SYNOPSIS
     sftp [-vC1] [-b batchfile] [-o ssh_option] [-s  subsystem  |
     sftp_server]    [-B   buffer_size]   [-F   ssh_config]   [-P
     sftp_server path] [-R num_requests] [-S program] host
     sftp [[user@]host[:file [file]]]
     sftp [[user@]host[:dir[/]]]

DESCRIPTION
     sftp is an interactive file  transfer  program,  similar  to
     ftp(1),  which  performs  all  operations  over an encrypted
     ssh(1) transport. It may also use  many  features  of  ssh,
     such  as  public  key  authentication and compression. sftp
     connects and logs into the specified host,  then  enters  an
     interactive command mode.

     The second usage format will retrieve files automatically if
--More--(13%)
```

You can use the Solaris `snoop` utility to verify that FTP does not encrypt communication and that `sftp` does encrypt – see Action 2.1.5 for examples of using the `snoop` utility.

Action 2.1.3 - Use the scp command as a replacement for "rcp" to exchange files with a remote system

The `scp` (secure copy) command is used to copy files and directories to and from remote servers. This command can be used as the replacement for the unencrypted rcp program. The `scp` command can also be used as a substitute for `sftp`, although there are some key differences.

One difference is that `scp` does not have an "interactive" mode as `sftp` does and therefore doesn't have as many capabilities, although it is still a quite powerful utility. One advantage of `scp` over `sftp` is that directory and recursive copies are much easier. Additionally, the `scp` command can be used in conjunction with an `.shosts` file to bypass interactive authentication – **this is strongly discouraged since it provides yet another avenue for attackers**. See Action 2.1.4 for more detail regarding host-based authentication with `.shosts` files.

So, if you have a need to copy directory entries in addition to files and/or you need to copy a directory structure recursively, `scp` is probably what you should use. If you're copying files only and they exist in multiple directories, or if you prefer interactivity, `sftp` is probably the better choice.

Although there are many options, the basic format of the `scp` command is as follows:

scp [options] [[user@]host1:]path-to-source [...] [[user2@]host2:]path-to-destination

Where:
    options = one of the valid options as referenced in the scp man page
    user = the account you are attempting to access on the remote system – if not specified, the current user name will be assumed.
    hostX = the remote system(s) to which you are attempting to copy to/from
    path-of-source = the source location of files/directories to copy
    path-of-destination = the destination location of files/directories to copy

The following example uses `scp` to duplicate the FTP file transfer from the last example (host is `server.example.com`, account is `sshuser`, file is `/tmp/snoop.txt`):

```
$ scp sshuser@server.example.com:/tmp/snoop.txt .
sshuser@server.example.com's password: ********
snoop.txt              100% |*****************************|  7956       00:00
$ ls -l
total 24
drwxr-xr-x   2 root      root        512  May 20  1999 103346-22
drwxr-xr-x   3 sshuser   150         512  Nov 10 09:39 ns_imap
drwx------   2 sshuser   150         512  Nov 10 09:39 nsmail
-rw-r--r--   1 sshuser   150        7956  Dec 18 14:30 snoop.txt
drwxrwxr-x   3 root      other       512  Jul 10  1999 upgrade
$
```

Besides the obvious advantage of encrypting communication, note that another advantage of `scp` over `rcp` is the verification of completion and the reporting of the number of bytes transferred.

You can also omit the user name as part of the command; if you do so, then the current user name will be assumed, as shown below:

```
$ scp server.example.com:/tmp/snoop.txt .
sshuser@server.example.com's password: *******
snoop.txt          100% |*****************************|  7956      00:00
$
```

In this example, we use the command line options -r to recursively copy a directory structure and -p to keep the original permissions of all files and directories:

```
$ scp -pr sshuser@server.example.com:/tmp/patches /tmp
sshuser@server.example.com's password: ********
105395-09.tar.Z  100% |*****************************| 537 KB 00:00
107684-09.zip    100% |*****************************| 851 KB 00:00
110615-09.zip    100% |*****************************| 868 KB 00:01
dsmerror.log     100% |*****************************| 150    00:00
```

The source directory is /tmp/patches, which is a directory with three subdirectories. The destination directory on the local machine is /tmp, so this command completely duplicates the /tmp/patches directory from host server.example.com to the local host, assuming your account has read permissions for all the files and directories in this structure. A *quick* way to verify that everything was copied is to use the du -sk command on both systems and compare the byte count, as shown below:

```
$ du -sk /tmp/patches
2284       /tmp/patches
```

Both systems should now report the same or roughly the same byte total. A more thorough method for verifying byte totals is to take checksums of files that were copied via scp. See the man pages for cksum, sum or other checksum utilities, depending on the flavor of UNIX you are using. Here's an example of using the cksum command:

```
$ find . -type f | xargs cksum
2795861523    550601    ./2.6/105395-09.tar.Z
405161581     872202    ./7/107684-09.zip
2165853569    889286    ./8/110615-09.zip
3510532143    150       ./8/dsmerror.log
```

Note that since we used the "-p" command line option to perform the copy, all permissions of the /tmp/patches and child sub-directories and files should be as they exist on the source system.

It should be noted that both sftp and scp can be utilized for "puts" as well as "gets" — all of the previous examples have demonstrated "gets". A "put" would be initiated from the machine where the data to be copied exists. The following example does the previous transfer in reverse, using "put" rather than "get":

```
$ scp -pr /tmp/patches sshuser@server.example.com:/tmp
sshuser@server.example.com's password: ********
105395-09.tar.Z      100% |*****************************| 537 KB    00:00
107684-09.zip        100% |*****************************| 851 KB    00:00
110615-09.zip        100% |*****************************| 868 KB    00:00
dsmerror.log         100% |*****************************| 150       00:00
$ uname -a
SunOS client.example.com 5.8 Generic_108528-16 sun4m sparc SUNW,SPARCstation-20
```

`scp` has many other command line options - to see them, issues `scp` with on options:

```
$ scp
usage: scp [-pqrvBC46] [-F config] [-S program] [-P port]
           [-c cipher] [-i identity] [-o option]
        [[user@]host1:]file1 [...] [[user@]host2:]file2
```

For more detail of each option, refer to the scp man page.

Action 2.1.4 - Use of Unix .rhosts /.shosts files for OpenSSH host-based authentication

Host-based authentication, with or without SSH, is considered a security danger in that it does not require interactive authentication (such as a password or passphrase). Host-based authentication is configured with various files to allow *automatic* (i.e. non-interactive) connections from one UNIX system to another. Since the use of UNIX host-based authentication is *strongly discouraged* from a security standpoint, the authors initially decided to simply mention the dangers of OpenSSH host-based authentication but not cover details for how to use it. However, we realized that in most environments, improving security via tools such as OpenSSH is rarely an "overnight" endeavor and therefore it is unrealistic to think that one can instantly eliminate the use of host-based authentication. We realize that while few will argue that host-based authentication is dangerous, it is also reality. Therefore, this section will briefly demonstrate OpenSSH's version of host-based authentication, although *it is important to note that utilizing OpenSSH with host-based authentication only improves security from the encrypted channel standpoint — it does not improve the authentication weakness inherent with host-based authentication.*

Normal UNIX host-based authentication is performed via the `/etc/hosts.equiv` file and `.rhosts` files. The `/etc/hosts.equiv` file should be considered the most dangerous and most easily abused method and should never be used — it performs authentication via client hostnames (or IP addresses) only. The `.rhosts` file performs authentication on a client hostname AND account name basis. OpenSSH can utilize existing `/etc/hosts.equiv` and `.rhosts` files as they exist for host-based authentication. OpenSSH can also utilize the `.shosts` file - which is simply an optional alternate name for `.rhosts` files. If you are currently utilizing an `.rhosts` file for host-based authentication, OpenSSH will also use that file once the host-based authentication is configured properly. You are not required to rename the `.rhosts` file to `.shosts`, although it may be a good idea to do so from the standpoint of users taking note of `.shosts` files and therefore realizing that SSH is in use on your server system.

OpenSSH host-based authentication requires configuration settings on both the SSH client machine (the one initiating the connection) and the server machine (the machine running the "sshd" daemon and performing the authentication).

> **Tech Tip**
> Each account on the SSH client can override settings in the OpenSSH system-wide configuration file (e.g. `/usr/local/etc/ssh_config`) by creating his/her own settings file in `$HOME/.ssh/config`. If a setting is not found in `$HOME/.ssh/config`, OpenSSH will then check the system-wide file. Configuration settings can also be specified on the command line. For example:
>
> ```
> $ ssh -o "ForwardX11 yes" -o "Compression yes" server.example.com
> Enter passphrase for key '/export/home/user_a/.ssh/id_rsa':
> ```
>
> command line options always override configuration file settings.

Client Settings

The following configuration option must be set as below in the /usr/local/etc/ssh_config file (assuming that OpenSSH was installed into /usr/local and that you are using SSHv2):

```
HostbasedAuthentication yes
```

(The corresponding setting for SSHv1 is "RhostsAuthentication")

Server Settings

1. The following configuration options must be set as below in the `/usr/local/etc/sshd_config` file (assuming that OpenSSH was installed in `/usr/local` and you are using SSHv2):

```
HostbasedAuthentication yes
IgnoreRhosts no
```

(The corresponding setting for host-based authentication for SSHv1 is "RhostsAuthentication")
Note that the comments in the `sshd_config` file say to *not* use Host-based authentication - use at your own risk!

2. Any SSH client that wishes to connect to this SSH server must be "known" - i.e., the clients' host keys must exist in the appropriate `known_hosts` file, either **`$HOME/.ssh/known_hosts`** for the server user account to which the connection will be made, or the system-wide `/usr/local/etc/sshd/ssh_known_hosts` file. An easy way to add the SSH client's host key to one of these files is to make an SSH connection from the server (which now temporarily becomes the SSH client) back to the client (temporarily the SSH server). Remember, you will have to first start the "sshd" daemon on the remote system before it will accept connections.

3. Create the `.rhosts` or `.shosts` file, if it doesn't already exist. There is no change in format for OpenSSH - use the same format as if you were performing host-based authentication without SSH. The `.rhosts/.shosts` file should contain one line for each remote client/account name combination that this server will allow to connect via host-based authentication. The first column contains the hostname, the second column is the account name. Spaces or tabs can separate the columns. Here is an example `.rhosts` file:

```
myclient            user_a
myclient.example.com user_a
```

Both entries here actually refer to the same machine/account - one is just fully qualified. This practice helps to eliminate problems with name resolution and host-based authentication.

4. The SSH server uses a reverse IP lookup as part of the host-based authentication procedure. Therefore, it is important that each portion of the configuration (`known_hosts`, `.rhosts`/`.shosts`, DNS or `/etc/host` file) utilize a consistent form for hostname verification/authentication - i.e. non-qualified (`myclient`) or fully-qualified (`myclient.example.com`). In many environments, DNS is the first entity used for hostname lookups. If DNS returns a fully qualified hostname, the SSH host-based authentication may fail, since the `known_hosts` file may have non-qualified hostname entries. Therefore you will also need to do *one* of two things in this regard to make sure that the SSH server can properly authenticate the SSH client:

   1. Modify the SSH server's /etc/hosts file to include an entry for the remote SSH client's IP address and hostname. Make sure that you have a non-qualified entry for the hostname so that it will match the hostname associated with the host in the known_hosts file ($HOME/.ssh/known_hosts or /usr/local/etc/ssh_known_hosts). For example, here is an /etc/hosts entry which includes both the non-qualified and fully-qualified hostnames:

      ```
      172.16.121.16    myclient    myclient.example.com
      ```

      Next, you may need to modify the SSH server's hostname lookup order, i.e., to search the local `/etc/host` file for hostname lookups BEFORE searching DNS, so that the non-qualified hostname will be returned. For many Unix versions, the file which controls this is `/etc/nsswitch.conf`. Following is a portion of that file modified for this example:

      ```
      passwd: files
       group: files
       hosts: files dns
      ipnodes: files
      ```

   OR

   2. Modify the SSH server's `known_hosts` file to utilize a fully-qualified domain name for the SSH client's host-key entry. Here is a modified entry:

      myclient.example.com,172.16.121.16 ssh-rsa AAAAB3NzaC1yc2EAAAABIwAAAIEAr7HxNPFUK2zWaLUSyi/ROby VPESK9X17HKLaiCKFsxEfvAc6fsLNfRVosQRLeuep/qR7ghbwscUB7PbRE1hK58aohXQUV/VXK1F4G4v P6wGNCfdwH9BjTrftDrEbzWprvaAD12fI1l+cjwydrp24+EQsIfHkcrwSP1ZRdk+3TDk=

Now that you've made all required host-based authentication configuration changes, you should be able to connect from the SSH client to the SSH server without having to enter a passphrase or password:

```
$ ssh -l sshuser server.example.com
Last login: Fri Apr 25 11:03:47 2003 from openv3
$ uname -a
SunOS kfs16 5.8 Generic_108528-06 sun4m sparc SUNW,SPARCstation-20
$
```

Here's another example, where a single host-based authenticated command is issued from the SSH client to the SSH server:

```
$ ssh -l sshuser server.example.com "ls -l"
total 3188
drwxr-xr-x   10 sshuser     admin        512       Dec 19 10:48 etc
-rw-r--r--    1 sshuser     admin        1620193 May 15 2002 openssh31.zip
```

Action 2.1.5 - Verify the SSH encryption

How can one be sure that the SSH session is indeed encrypted? UNIX/Linux systems provide various network packet inspection utilities which verify — to a certain extent — that the transmitted data is encrypted. Following are two examples of connections that are "sniffed" by the Solaris snoop utility – the first shows a clear-text telnet session while the second shows an encrypted SSH session. TCPDUMP and Ethereal are functionally similar open-source tools which you might also consider for this purpose.

Example 1 – Snoop output of telnet session

- First, we'll need to login to the root account on the telnet server (`server.example.com`) since the snoop utility requires root permissions. Issue the following snoop command to start capturing network connection information originating from the SSH client machine (`client.example.com`) and related to port 23 (which is the default telnet port):

    ```
    $ su -
    Password: ********
    # snoop -o /tmp/snoop.txt port 23 client.example.com
    Using device /dev/le (promiscuous mode)
    0
    ```

This command saves all the snoop output into a file for later viewing. In the next step, we'll connect from the client via telnet and the packet counter (the 0 shown above) should start increasing to reflect that packets are being captured.

- Next, open a telnet connection to the server from the client, then immediately exit, as shown below:

    ```
    $ telnet server.example.com
    Trying 172.16.121.6...
    Connected to server.example.com
    Escape character is '^]'.

    SunOS 5.8

    login: sshuser
    Password: *******
    Last login: Sat Apr 12 19:03:52 from 172.16.122.159
    $ exit
    ```

- Now go back to the server session and press CTRL+C to abort the snoop packet capturing. The packet counter displayed by snoop should have incremented, reflecting the number of packets it has "captured" from the network traffic. Use the following command to read what snoop captured:

    ```
    # snoop -i /tmp/snoop.txt | more
    ```

    (some output cut for brevity)

    ```
         3    0.00078 client.example.com -> server.example.com TELNET C port=33861
         4    0.02125 client.example.com -> server.example.com TELNET C port=33861
         5    0.00008 server.example.com -> client.example.com TELNET R port=33861
         6    0.28402 server.example.com -> client.example.com TELNET R port=33861
         7    0.00069 client.example.com -> server.example.com TELNET C port=33861
         8    0.00043 server.example.com -> client.example.com TELNET R port=33861
         9    0.00028 client.example.com -> server.example.com TELNET C port=33861
        10    0.09378 server.example.com -> client.example.com TELNET R port=33861
        11    0.00028 client.example.com -> server.example.com TELNET C port=33861
        12    0.00008 server.example.com -> client.example.com TELNET R port=33861
        13    0.00386 client.example.com -> server.example.com TELNET C port=33861 \377\3
    72\30\0VT320\377\360\377\372#\0openv
        14    0.02279 server.example.com -> client.example.com TELNET R port=33861
        15    0.09331 client.example.com -> server.example.com TELNET C port=33861
        16    0.00014 server.example.com -> client.example.com TELNET R port=33861
        17    0.00158 client.example.com -> server.example.com TELNET C port=33861
        18    0.00048 server.example.com -> client.example.com TELNET R port=33861
        19    0.09758 client.example.com -> server.example.com TELNET C port=33861
        20    4.28797 server.example.com -> client.example.com TELNET R port=33861 ******
    **************
        21    0.09277 client.example.com -> server.example.com TELNET C port=33861
        22    0.00027 server.example.com -> client.example.com TELNET R port=33861

        23    0.09940 client.example.com -> server.example.com TELNET C port=33861
        24    0.78898 client.example.com -> server.example.com TELNET C port=33861 s
        25    0.00031 server.example.com -> client.example.com TELNET R port=33861 s
        26    0.10070 client.example.com -> server.example.com TELNET C port=33861
        27    0.19873 client.example.com -> server.example.com TELNET C port=33861 s
        28    0.00037 server.example.com -> client.example.com TELNET R port=33861 s
        29    0.01794 client.example.com -> server.example.com TELNET C port=33861 h
        30    0.00024 server.example.com -> client.example.com TELNET R port=33861 h
        31    0.09264 client.example.com -> server.example.com TELNET C port=33861
        32    0.18913 client.example.com -> server.example.com TELNET C port=33861 u
    ```

```
33   0.00033 server.example.com -> client.example.com TELNET R port=33861 u
34   0.03462 client.example.com -> server.example.com TELNET C port=33861 s
35   0.00026 server.example.com -> client.example.com TELNET R port=33861 s
36   0.09568 client.example.com -> server.example.com TELNET C port=33861
37   0.17001 client.example.com -> server.example.com TELNET C port=33861 e
38   0.00035 server.example.com -> client.example.com TELNET R port=33861 e
39   0.07298 client.example.com -> server.example.com TELNET C port=33861 r
40   0.00047 server.example.com -> client.example.com TELNET R port=33861 r
41   0.09634 client.example.com -> server.example.com TELNET C port=33861
42   0.00008 server.example.com -> client.example.com TELNET R port=33861 Password:
43   0.09982 client.example.com -> server.example.com TELNET C port=33861
44   1.47820 client.example.com -> server.example.com TELNET C port=33861 B
45   0.09170 server.example.com -> client.example.com TELNET R port=33861
46   0.14235 client.example.com -> server.example.com TELNET C port=33861 ony
47   0.09765 server.example.com -> client.example.com TELNET R port=33861
48   0.19136 client.example.com -> server.example.com TELNET C port=33861 9t
49   0.09859 server.example.com -> client.example.com TELNET R port=33861
50   0.23350 client.example.com -> server.example.com TELNET C port=33861 o
51   0.09662 server.example.com -> client.example.com TELNET R port=33861
52   0.01480 client.example.com -> server.example.com TELNET C port=33861 e
53   0.09507 server.example.com -> client.example.com TELNET R port=33861
```

Note the ASCII representation of the dialogue in the far right column. You can see that in this example, the account name and password are in clear-text and easy to detect! This is why telnet and FTP are called "clear-text" utilities – all communication is sent over the network in clear-text.

Example 2 – Snoop output of SSH session

- Now that we know how to use snoop, we can snoop the output of an SSH session and demonstrate that it is encrypted. First, start the snoop session on the server, looking for traffic from client `client.example.com` and port 22 (which is the default SSH port), as shown below:
  ```
  # snoop -o /tmp/snoop.txt port 22 client.example.com
  Using device /dev/le (promiscuous mode
  0
  ```

- Next, connect via OpenSSH from the client machine and issue an `ls` command, as shown below:
  ```
  $ ssh -l sshuser server.example.com
  sshuser@server.example.com's password:
  Last login: Mon Apr 14 11:13:12 2003 from client.example.com.
  $ ls
  a              etc          nsmail        openssh31.zip
  $
  ```

- Now go back to the server session and press CTRL+C to abort the snoop packet capturing.
- Use the following command to read what snoop captured:
  ```
  # snoop -i /tmp/snoop.txt | more
  ```

  (some output cut for brevity)

  ```
    1   0.00000 client.example.com -> server.example.com TCP D=22 S=33874 Syn Seq=161238050 Len=0 Win=24820 Options=<nop,nop,sackOK,mss 1460>
    2   0.00003 server.example.com -> client.example.com TCP D=33874 S=22 Syn Ack=161238051 Seq=3683871110 Len=0 Win=24820 Options=<nop,nop,sackOK,mss 1460>
    3   0.00097 client.example.com -> server.example.com TCP D=22 S=33874     Ack=3683871111 Seq=161238051 Len=0 Win=24820
    4   0.07606 server.example.com -> client.example.com TCP D=33874 S=22     Ack=161238051 Seq=3683871111 Len=22 Win=24820
    5   0.00067 client.example.com -> server.example.com TCP D=22 S=33874     Ack=3683871133 Seq=161238051 Len=0 Win=24820
    6   0.19015 client.example.com -> server.example.com TCP D=22 S=33874     Ack=3683871133 Seq=161238051 Len=22 Win=24820
    7   0.00007 server.example.com -> client.example.com TCP D=33874 S=22     Ack=161238073 Seq=3683871133 Len=0 Win=24820
    8   0.01781 client.example.com -> server.example.com TCP D=22 S=33874     Ack=3683871133 Seq=161238073 Len=544 Win=24820
    9   0.07882 server.example.com -> client.example.com TCP D=33874 S=22     Ack=161238617 Seq=3683871133 Len=544 Win=24820
   10   0.01344 client.example.com -> server.example.com TCP D=22 S=33874     Ack=3683871677 Seq=161238617 Len=24 Win=24820
   11   0.09352 server.example.com -> client.example.com TCP D=33874 S=22     Ack=161238641 Seq=3683871677 Len=0 Win=24820
   12   0.05308 server.example.com -> client.example.com TCP D=33874 S=22     Ack=161238641 Seq=3683871677 Len=424 Win=24820
   13   0.09536 client.example.com -> server.example.com TCP D=22 S=33874     Ack=3683872101 Seq=161238641 Len=0 Win=24820
   14   0.74769 client.example.com -> server.example.com TCP D=22 S=33874     Ack=3683872101 Seq=161238641 Len=416 Win=24820
   15   0.09385 server.example.com -> client.example.com TCP D=33874 S=22     Ack=161239057 Seq=3683872101 Len=0 Win=24820
   16   1.00661 server.example.com -> client.example.com TCP D=33874 S=22     Ack=161239057 Seq=3683872101 Len=736 Win=24820
  ```

```
   17    0.10202 client.example.com -> server.example.com TCP D=22 S=33874      Ack=3
683872837 Seq=161239057 Len=0 Win=24820
   18    0.96630 client.example.com -> server.example.com TCP D=22 S=33874      Ack=3
683872837 Seq=161239057 Len=16 Win=24820
   19    0.09513 server.example.com -> client.example.com TCP D=33874 S=22      Ack=1
61239073 Seq=3683872837 Len=0 Win=24820
   20    0.00081 client.example.com -> server.example.com TCP D=22 S=33874      Ack=3
683872837 Seq=161239073 Len=48 Win=24820
   21    0.04351 server.example.com -> client.example.com TCP D=33874 S=22      Ack=1
61239121 Seq=3683872837 Len=48 Win=24820
```

Note that in this snoop output, there is no readable data in the far right-hand column, since all the data is encrypted.

- For a more thorough analysis of the network packets, you can use the "-x 0" parameter to snoop that will display data in both hex and ASCII format. Note the encryption-related detail displayed in the far right column:

```
# snoop -i /tmp/snoop.txt -x 0 | more

(some output cut for brevity)

         0:  0800 2077 0121 0800 207a 6ae5 0800 4500    .. w.!.. zj...E.
        16:  0028 d071 4000 4006 2027 ac10 7906 ac10    .(.q@.@. '..y...
        32:  7910 0016 8452 db93 699d 099c 4c39 5010    y....R..i...L9P.
        48:  60f4 e539 0000                             `..9..

    8    0.01781 client.example.com -> server.example.com TCP D=22 S=33874      Ack=3
683871133 Seq=161238073 Len=544 Win=24820

         0:  0800 207a 6ae5 0800 2077 0121 0800 4500    .. zj... w.!..E.
        16:  0248 684f 4000 4006 8629 ac10 7910 ac10    .HhO@.@..)..y...
        32:  7906 8452 0016 099c 4c39 db93 699d 5018    y..R....L9..i.P.
        48:  60f4 8725 0000 0000 021c 0914 b507 d790    `..%............
        64:  8d12 568c 6627 7c75 9487 347b 0000 003d    ..V.f'|u..4{...=
        80:  6469 6666 6965 2d68 656c 6c6d 616e 2d67    diffie-hellman-g
        96:  726f 7570 2d65 7863 6861 6e67 652d 7368    roup-exchange-sh
       112:  6131 2c64 6966 6669 652d 6865 6c6c 6d61    a1,diffie-hellma
       128:  6e2d 6772 6f75 7031 2d73 6861 3100 0000    n-group1-sha1...
       144:  0f73 7368 2d72 7361 2c73 7368 2d64 7373    .ssh-rsa,ssh-dss
       160:  0000 0066 6165 7331 3238 2d63 6263 2c33    ...faes128-cbc,3
```

```
176: 6465 732d 6362 632c 626c 6f77 6669 7368     des-cbc,blowfish
192: 2d63 6263 2c63 6173 7431 3238 2d63 6263     -cbc,cast128-cbc
208: 2c61 7263 666f 7572 2c61 6573 3139 322d     ,arcfour,aes192-
224: 6362 632c 6165 7332 3536 2d63 6263 2c72     cbc,aes256-cbc,r
240: 696a 6e64 6165 6c2d 6362 6340 6c79 7361     ijndael-cbc@lysa
256: 746f 722e 6c69 752e 7365 0000 0066 6165     tor.liu.se...fae
272: 7331 3238 2d63 6263 2c33 6465 732d 6362     s128-cbc,3des-cb
288: 632c 626c 6f77 6669 7368 2d63 6263 2c63     c,blowfish-cbc,c
304: 6173 7431 3238 2d63 6263 2c61 7263 666f     ast128-cbc,arcfo
320: 7572 2c61 6573 3139 322d 6362 632c 6165     ur,aes192-cbc,ae
336: 7332 3536 2d63 6263 2c72 696a 6e64 6165     s256-cbc,rijndae
352: 6c2d 6362 6340 6c79 7361 746f 722e 6c69     l-cbc@lysator.li
368: 752e 7365 0000 0055 686d 6163 2d6d 6435     u.se...Uhmac-md5
384: 2c68 6d61 632d 7368 6131 2c68 6d61 632d     ,hmac-sha1,hmac-
400: 7269 7065 6d64 3136 302c 686d 6163 2d72     ripemd160,hmac-r
416: 6970 656d 6431 3630 406f 7065 6e73 7368     ipemd160@openssh
```

Section 3 - How To Use PuTTY/WinSCP For PC-To-UNIX Connectivity

Problem: Now that PuTTY is installed, we need to learn how to utilize it for invoking remote interactive connections from a Windows host to a UNIX server running OpenSSH.

Step 3.1 Use PuTTY as a Graphical Replacement for telnet and rlogin

Action 3.1.1 – Configure PuTTY to connect to a remote machine

Now that PuTTY is installed, it can be used to connect to remote machines running the OpenSSH server. The graphical component of PuTTY is used to connect to remote machines and create a telnet or rlogin-like shell session.

- First, double-click on the icon that was created for PuTTY or select it from the **Start Menu** to start the program. A window will display as shown below. This is where the configuration of each SSH session can be changed.

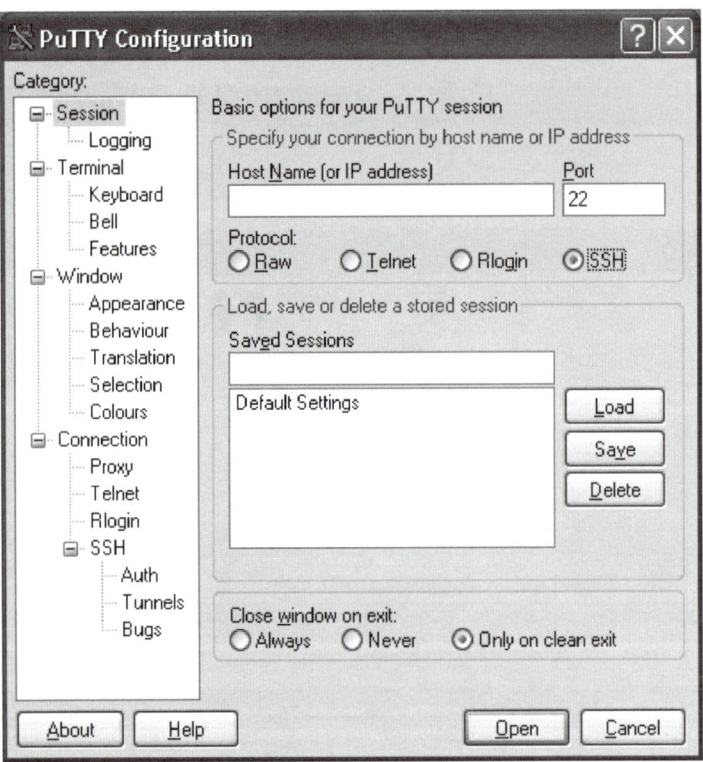

On the left side of the configuration window is a list of categories. Clicking on any of the categories will display in the right-hand window the different options that are configurable for the SSH session. PuTTY comes with a very useful help file that describes each of the options in detail. Except for the SSH version specification, the default for each option is reasonable and secure, so the majority of them should not have to be changed.

SSH version 1 has known weaknesses and should be avoided. Select SSH version 2 **only** by clicking on the SSH category and selecting 2 only from the **Preferred SSH protocol version**, as shown below.

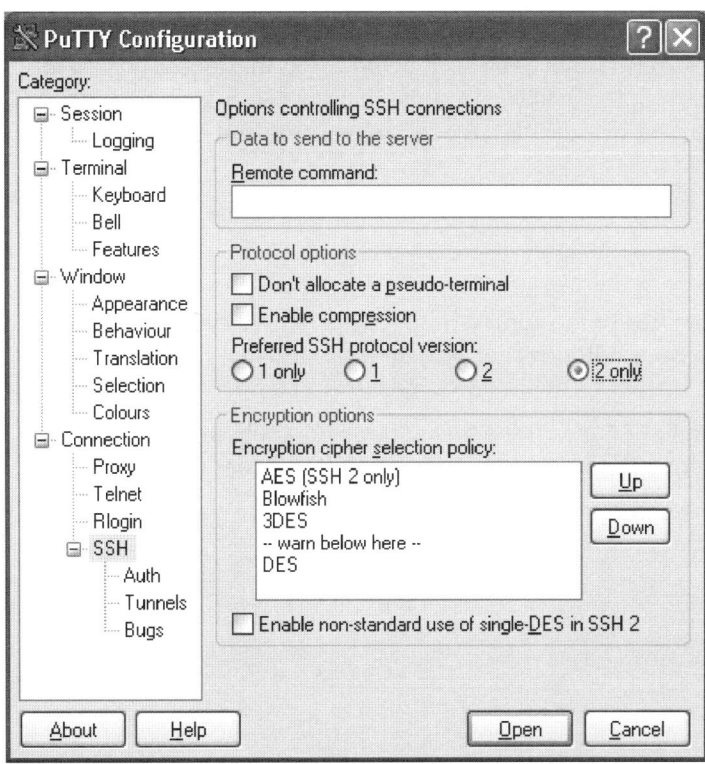

- If it is not already selected, click once on the Session category. This will display the most basic options that need to be configured for the SSH session.

The upper section of the window will display an entry for the Host Name or IP address of the machine to which you wish to connect, the Port Number on which the service is listening and which protocol to use. Since we want to create an SSH session, make sure SSH is selected and type in the Host Name or IP address of the machine to which you wish to connect. Leave the Port Number set to 22 as this is SSH's default port.

> *OPTIONAL: Below the connection settings is an area where you can load, save or delete sessions.*
> *To save a session, type a name for the session in the area below the **Saved Sessions** text and click on the **Save** button.*
> *The name you have given the session will appear and can now be recalled by either double-clicking on the name*
> *or selecting the name and clicking on the **Load** button. This is to provide a way to quickly recall settings for specific sessions.*

- Once the hostname or IP address of the machine to which you wish to connect has been entered, click on the **Open** button at the bottom of the window. The configuration windows will disappear and PuTTY will attempt to connect to the machine you specified.

If PuTTY is successful, a terminal window with an empty black background and a PuTTY Security Alert, as shown below, will appear. The security alert is telling you that you have not connected to this machine before and the machine's host key has not been seen before. This message is normal for the first time connecting to a server via SSH. *After* you contact the administrator or a user of the machine to verify that the server's key fingerprint is correct, click the **Yes** button. The administrator or user can verify the server's key fingerprint by executing the following command on the server:

```
$ ssh-keygen -l -f file
```

Where `file` is the name of the host's public SSH key, such as `/etc/ssh/ssh_host_key.pub`. The result will look similar to the following and should match the key fingerprint previously given:

```
1024 7d:7a:5b:55:0a:20:46:65:07:04:b4:b5:60:d3:82:1e
```

Keep in mind that the fingerprint *must* be transmitted in a secure manner (i.e. by a phone call to the administrator of the remote system), since SSH relies on these keys and the fingerprint is the simple proof for a valid key. For obvious reasons, SSH does not provide a way to fetch such fingerprints remotely from an SSH server.

- You should only see this message the first time you successfully connect to a server with PuTTY. If you see the message on a subsequent attempt, something is wrong -- see action 5.2.6 for possible security risks. Also, if you get a dialogue stating that "the cached host key does not match" see action 5.2.7.

If the connection is not successful, a black window will appear after you click the **Open** button, but instead of the expected PuTTY security alert, a timeout error will appear.

- After you click the **Yes** button in the security alert window, the black window will display user ID and password prompts. If you enter your authentication information correctly, you will receive a shell prompt. You are now connected to the remote machine.

Problem: Even though most work within Windows is done through a graphical interface, there are times when it is necessary to create an SSH session from a Windows command prompt or from within a script.

Step 3.2 Use PuTTY / plink as a Command Line Replacement for telnet / rlogin

Action 3.2.1 Create an SSH session from the command line using PuTTY

There are multiple ways to create an SSH session from the command line using PuTTY.

The first way involves using the PuTTY program itself. PuTTY comes with a number of options that can be used to invoke the graphical PuTTY terminal from the command line. A description of these options is available within the PuTTY help file. To run PuTTY from the command line:

> *Note: For any command line PuTTY program to work, the Windows PATH environment variable must be set to include the path to the directory in which the PuTTY programs are installed.*

- Click on the **Start Menu** and select **Run**. In the field provided, type in `cmd` if you are running Windows NT/2000/XP or `command` if you are running Windows 9x/ME and click on the **OK** button. This will give you a Windows command prompt.
- From the command prompt, invoke PuTTY using the following syntax:

putty –ssh [**-l** *user*] [*user@*]*hostname*

Where:
> *user* = the account you are trying to access on the remote machine.
> *hostname* = the hostname or IP address of the machine you are trying to contact.

PuTTY also allows you to open a saved session from the command line. To do this, use one of the following arguments at the command line:

putty –load "*session name*"

putty @"*session name*"

Where:
> *session name* = the name of the saved session. (If the session name contains spaces, it should be surrounded by quotes.)

For example, if you want to start PuTTY with a connection to server.example.com as user sshuser, type the following at the Windows command prompt and press **Enter**:

```
C:\>putty -ssh -l sshuser server.example.com
```

To start PuTTY with a saved session called "ssh server", type the following at the Windows command prompt and press **Enter**:

```
C:\>putty -load "ssh server"
```

After authenticating successfully, you will have a shell prompt on the remote machine.

Action 3.2.2 Using Plink to initiate an SSH session from the command line or a script

Using PuTTY from the command line as in the way described in the previous section will create an SSH interactive session. This may not be what we want if for example we need to remain at the Windows command line or we want to issue an SSH command from within a script. In order to satisfy these types of needs, PuTTY provides a tool called Plink.

- Plink is a command line tool that will allow you to log in to a remote machine using SSH and either create an SSH session or execute a command, all from the command line and without opening another window. Plink comes with many command line options that can be accessed with the -h option:

```
C:\>plink -h
PuTTY Link: command line connection utility
Release 0.53b
Usage: plink [options] [user@]host [command]
       ("host" can also be a PuTTY saved session name)
Options:
  -v        show verbose messages
  -load sessname  Load settings from saved session
  -ssh -telnet -rlogin -raw
            force use of a particular protocol (default SSH)
  -P port   connect to specified port
  -l user   connect with specified username
  -m file   read remote command(s) from file
  -batch    disable all interactive prompts
The following options only apply to SSH connections:
  -pw passw login with specified password
  -L listen-port:host:port   Forward local port to remote address
  -R listen-port:host:port   Forward remote port to local address
  -X -x     enable / disable X11 forwarding
  -A -a     enable / disable agent forwarding
  -t -T     enable / disable pty allocation
  -1 -2     force use of particular protocol version
  -C        enable compression
  -i key    private key file for authentication
```

However, you will probably never use many of the options available. The most common options you will likely use are as follows:
plink [**-v**] [**-batch**] [**-l** *user*] [*-load session*] [*user@*]*hostname* [*command*]

where:
-*l user* = the account you are trying to access on the remote machine.
hostname = the hostname or IP address of the machine you are trying to contact
command = optional command you want Plink to execute on the remote machine. If no command is specified, an SSH session will be created.
-*v* = enables verbose mode. This is helpful when something is awry and you want more information about the connection.
-*batch* = disables interactive prompts when Plink is establishing a connection. This is useful when you are running Plink within a script. If an interactive prompt appears during connection, Plink will fail the connection rather than hang.
-*load session* = the name of the saved PuTTY session to load. This is used as an alternative to giving Plink a user and hostname with which to connect.

To run Plink:

- If you are not already at a Windows command prompt, click on the **Start Menu** and select **Run**. In the field provided, type in cmd if you are running Windows NT/2000/XP or command if you are running Windows 9x/ME and click on the **OK** button. This will give you a Windows command prompt.

- From the Windows command prompt, issue the plink command. For example, to establish a connection to remote host server.example.com as user sshuser:
  ```
  C:\>plink -ssh sshuser@server.example.com
  sshuser@server.example.com's password: *******
  Last login: Thu Jan  9 10:40:13 2003 from 192.168.1.10
  $
  ```

In this case, Plink opens up an SSH session from the local machine to the remote host just as PuTTY would.

> **NOTE:** *Running an SSH connection from within a Windows command prompt may result in undesirable effects, due to the fact that the Windows command prompt does not know how to handle the control codes from the different terminal types that are set up in a remote UNIX shell session. Therefore, running commands such as* clear *may cause garbage to display on the screen. If possible, use PuTTY to open a shell session to a remote machine.*

Plink can also be used to create an SSH session and execute a command or script on the remote machine from the Windows command line. For example, to connect to remote host server.example.com as user sshuser to run the command uname –a:
```
C:\>plink -ssh sshuser@server.example.com "uname -a"
sshuser@server.example.com's password: ********
Linux server.example.com 2.4.7-10smp #1 SMP Thu Sep 6 17:09:31 EDT 2001 i686 unknown

C:\>
```

As you can see, Plink connects to the remote machine, is prompted for authentication, and upon successful authentication executes the command provided and displays any output on the local machine.

Problem: Working in a shell on a remote server is great, but what happens when you need to securely transfer files? This is where WinSCP comes in.

Step 3.3 Use WinSCP as a Graphical Replacement for FTP and RCP

Action 3.3.1 – Use WinSCP to connect to a remote machine

- Double-click on the WinSCP icon or select WinSCP from the Windows **Start Menu** to launch the program. The WinSCP connection window will display as shown below:

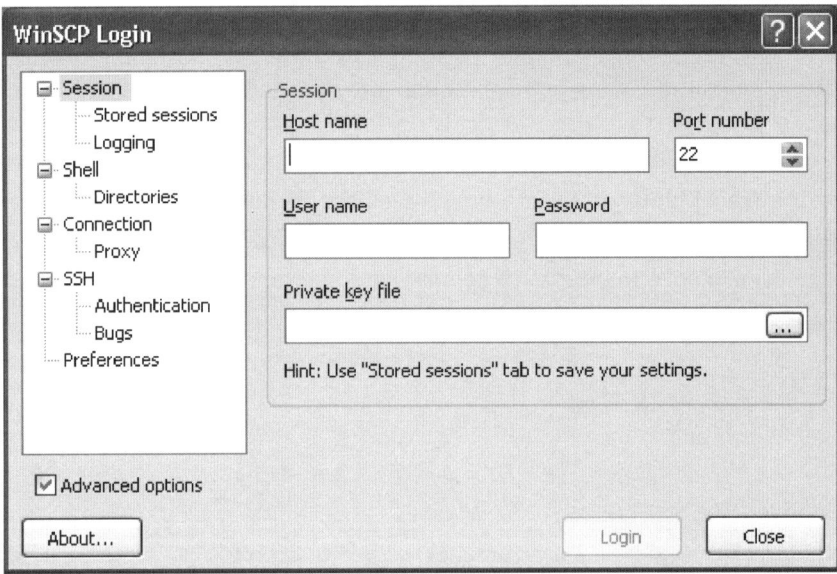

- Within the displayed window, enter the hostname or IP address of the machine to which you wish to connect in the **Host Name** field, the user ID of the user you will be connecting as in the **User name** field, and the password associated with this user ID in the **Password** field. Leave the **Port number** field value at "22", unless your remote OpenSSH server is listening on a different port. The **Private key file** field can be left blank. After all information is entered, click on the **Login** button.

- WinSCP will then try to connect to the remote machine using SSH. If your authentication information was not correct, you will be asked to re-enter your password or passphrase.

- If the connection is successful and this is the first connection to the remote machine, a warning, as shown below, will be displayed. You should contact the administrator of the server to which you are connecting and verify the server's key fingerprint. This is discussed in Action 3.1.1.

USE WINSCP AS A GRAPHICAL REPLACEMENT FOR FTP AND RCP 45

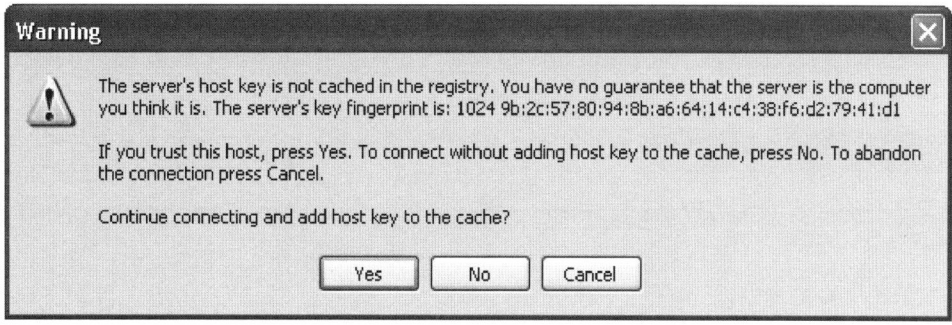

- After you have verified the server's fingerprint, click the **Yes** button; if you have authenticated successfully, you will be presented with a view of the remote machine, depending on what interface style you chose. If you chose the Norton Commander-style, two side-by-side windows, as shown below, will appear. On the left will be a directory listing of your local machine. On the right will be a directory listing of the remote machine to which you are connected. You are now ready to transfer files.

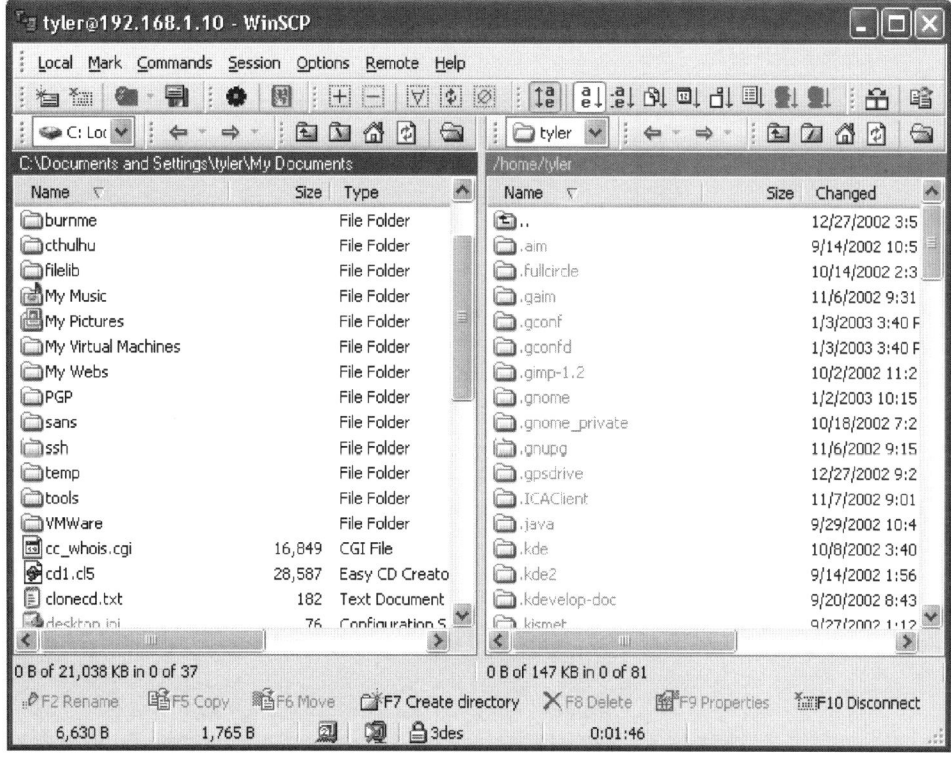

In order to transfer a file from one machine to another, you drag and drop the file from one window to another.

- If you chose the Windows Explorer-style interface, a window similar to the one shown below will appear. This is the current directory on the remote machine.

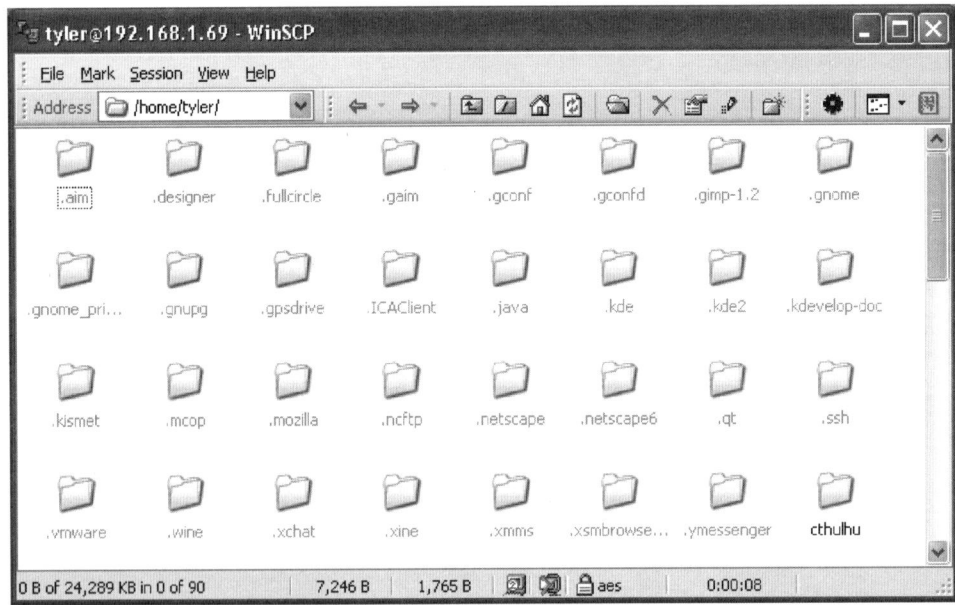

- In order to transfer a file from one machine to another, open up Windows Explorer on the local machine, find the file to copy and drag it into the WinSCP window. The file will transfer to the remote machine. To transfer a file from the remote machine to the local host, simply click on the file in the WinSCP window and drag it into Windows Explorer. Alternatively, double-clicking on a file on the remote server will automatically copy it to the default local folder, which can be configured in the **Shell->Directories->Local Directory** field of WinSCP's advanced options.

Problem: Something is needed to replace the insecure FTP and rcp Windows command line utilities.

Step 3.4 Use PuTTY's Tools to Transfer Files from the Windows Command Line

Action 3.4.1 Interactively transfer files from the command line with PSFTP

- One method to transfer files from the Windows command line is to use PSFTP. PSFTP creates an interactive SFTP file transfer session where you can use many of the commands available within a normal FTP session. Since PSFTP uses the SFTP protocol, which is only available with servers running protocol SSHv2, you may not be able to run it on every server.

PSFTP is run from the command line and provides numerous options. To see the options available run PSFTP with the –h option:

```
C:\>psftp -h
PuTTY Secure File Transfer (SFTP) client
Release 0.53b
Usage: psftp [options] user@host
Options:
  -b file   use specified batchfile
  -bc       output batchfile commands
  -be       don't stop batchfile processing if errors
  -v        show verbose messages
  -load sessname  Load settings from saved session
  -l user   connect with specified username
  -P port   connect to specified port
  -pw passw login with specified password
  -1 -2     force use of particular SSH protocol version
  -C        enable compression
  -i key    private key file for authentication
  -batch    disable all interactive prompts
```

- Once you have started PSFTP, you will be placed into the PSFTP shell where you can connect to a remote machine (if you have not already done so), transfer files and modify file and directory attributes. To view a list of the commands available and what they do, run the help command from within the PSFTP shell:

```
psftp> help
!     run a local Windows command
bye   finish your SFTP session
cd    change your remote working directory
chmod change file permissions and modes
del   delete a file
dir   list contents of a remote directory
exit  finish your SFTP session
```

```
get    download a file from the server to your local machine
help   give help
lcd    change local working directory
lpwd   print local working directory
ls     list contents of a remote directory
mkdir  create a directory on the remote server
mv     move or rename a file on the remote server
open   connect to a host
put    upload a file from your local machine to the server
pwd    print your remote working directory
quit   finish your SFTP session
reget  continue downloading a file
ren    move or rename a file on the remote server
reput  continue uploading a file
rm     delete a file
rmdir  remove a directory on the remote server
```

The following is an example PSFTP session showing how to connect to remote server `server.example.com` as user `sshuser` and transfer files.

- Click on the **Start Menu** and select **Run**. In the field provided, type in `cmd` if you are running Windows NT/2000/XP or `command` if you are running Windows 9x/ME and click on the **OK** button.

- Next, type `psftp` at the command line and you will be placed into a PSFTP shell. Remember, you must have the path to the PuTTY executables defined within your Windows environment variable "PATH" in order for this to work.
  ```
  C:\> psftp
  psftp: no hostname specified; use "open host.name" to connect
  psftp>
  ```

- Open a connection to the remote machine by invoking the `open` command with the following syntax:
  open [*user@*]*hostname*

  where `user` is the optional user ID you will connect to the remote machine as and `hostname` is the name or IP address of the host to which you will connect. You can alternatively specify the remote host and user name when invoking PSFTP from the command line.

  If you have not connected to this machine previously, you may be asked whether or not you want to cache the host key.

  Once the connection to the machine is open, you will be prompted for authentication. Upon successful authentication, the connection to the remote machine will have completed and the transfer of files can begin.
  ```
  psftp> open sshuser@server.example.com
  Using username "sshuser".
  sshuser@server.example.com's password: ********
  Remote working directory is /home/sshuser
  psftp>
  ```

- Next, you should verify the current local directory. This is done with the `lpwd` command. If you are not within the correct directory, the current local directory can be changed with the `lcd` command which takes a directory name as its argument. For example:
  ```
  psftp> lpwd
  Current local directory is C:\
  psftp> lcd c:\temp
  New local directory is c:\temp
  psftp> lpwd
  Current local directory is c:\temp
  psftp>
  ```

- Once you are within the correct local directory, you can change to the correct directory on the remote machine. This is done using the `pwd` and `cd` commands. The `pwd` command will print the remote connection's current directory and `cd` will change the remote connection to the directory provided as an argument.
  ```
  psftp> pwd
  Remote directory is /home/sshuser
  psftp> cd /tmp
  Remote directory is now /tmp
  psftp>
  ```

- Now that you are within the correct remote directory, you can verify that the file to download is present. This is done using the `dir` command. The `dir` command will display a UNIX-style listing of the current remote directory:

> *Note: For those familiar with UNIX, the "ls" command can be used in place of "dir".*
> *Use the "help" command to see a full listing of commands available.*

```
psftp> dir
Listing directory /tmp
drwx------    2 root       root           1024 Jan  9 14:07 .
drwxr-xr-x    8 root       root           1024 Jan  9 14:06 ..
-rw-r--r--    1 root       root            124 Jan  9 14:06 test.c
-rw-r--r--    1 root       root           3511 Jan  9 14:06 test.C
-rw-r--r--    1 sshuser    sshuser         151 Jan  9 14:07 test.pl
psftp>
```

- Use the `get` command to download remote files. The `get` command's syntax is as follows:

get *remote-filename* [*local-filename*]

where `remote-filename` is the name of the file you wish to download. You can optionally specify a new name for the downloaded file with the `local-filename` argument:
  ```
  psftp> get test.pl
  remote:/tmp/test.pl => local:test.pl
  psftp>
  ```

- You have seen the PSFTP `lpwd` command to show the current local directory and the `lcd` command to change the current local directory, but there are no commands to see the contents of the local directory. To accomplish this, you can use the "`!`" command. The "`!`" command will execute the supplied OS command and receive and display whatever output is returned.

  So, in order to see if a file you wish to upload is present in the current local directory - test.sh in this case - we will use the "`!`" command with `dir test.sh` as its arguments.

  ```
  psftp> !dir test.sh
   Volume in drive C has no label.
   Volume Serial Number is 1234-ABCD

   Directory of C:\temp

  07/10/02  03:03p                     165 test.sh
                 1 File(s)             165 bytes
                               4,577,963,520 bytes free
  psftp>
  ```

- You can upload files to the remote server using the `put` command. The syntax for the `put` command is as follows:

  put *local-filename* [*remote-filename*]

  where `local-filename` is the name of the file you wish to upload. You can also optionally specify a new name for the file to be uploaded as with the `remote-filename` argument.

  ```
  psftp> put test.sh
  local:test.sh => remote:/tmp/test.sh
  psftp> dir
  Listing directory /tmp
  drwxrwxrwt   2 root     root         1024 Jan  9 14:07 .
  drwxr-xr-x   8 root     root         1024 Jan  9 14:06 ..
  -rw-r--r--   1 root     root          124 Jan  9 14:06 test.c
  -rw-r--r--   1 root     root         3511 Jan  9 14:06 test.C
  -rw-r--r--   1 sshuser  sshuser       151 Jan  9 14:07 test.pl
  -rw-rw-r--   1 sshuser  sshuser       165 Jan  9 14:37 test.sh
  psftp>
  ```

- To close down a PSFTP connection, issue the `bye` command and you will be returned to the Windows command prompt:

  ```
  psftp> bye

  C:\>
  ```

Action 3.4.2 Transfer files from the command line with PSCP

A second method to transfer files from a Windows command line prompt is to use PSCP. Unlike PSFTP, PSCP is not interactive and is designed to transfer files "in one shot" and then exit, much like OpenSSH's scp command. PSCP also allows you to specify wildcards within filenames (PSFTP does not). Additionally, PSCP will work with any SSH server as it is not dependent on SSHv2 being present.

> *Note: PSCP will blindly copy files to the remote server, overwriting any files with the same name, without prompting for verification. Be careful when using PSCP to copy files.*
>
> *If you wish to prevent PSCP from overwriting any files, remove any write permissions on any file you wish to keep. This can be done on a UNIX system by issuing the following command:*
>
> $ chmod -w file
>
> *This will prevent PSCP from overwriting the file.*

PSCP is run from the command line and has many options, which you can see via the -h option:

```
C:\>pscp -h
PuTTY Secure Copy client
Release 0.53b
Usage:     pscp [options] [user@]host:source target
           pscp [options] source [source...] [user@]host:target
           pscp [options] -ls user@host:filespec
Options:
  -p           preserve file attributes
  -q           quiet, don't show statistics
  -r           copy directories recursively
  -v           show verbose messages
  -load sessname  Load settings from saved session
  -P port      connect to specified port
  -l user      connect with specified username
  -pw passw    login with specified password
  -1 -2        force use of particular SSH protocol version
  -C           enable compression
  -i key       private key file for authentication
  -batch       disable all interactive prompts
  -unsafe      allow server-side wildcards (DANGEROUS)
```

Some of the more common options are explained in more detail below:

-*p* = This will preserve the date and timestamps on any file transferred.

-*r* = By default, PSCP will only copy files and skip over any directories encountered. The -r option will recursively copy any directory structures encountered.

The following are two examples of utilizing PSCP to exchange files with machine `server.example.com` as user `sshuser`.

- Click on the **Start Menu** and select **Run**. In the field provided, type in `cmd` if you are running Windows NT/2000/XP or `command` if you are running Windows 9x/ME and click on the **OK** button.

The syntax for downloading a file from a remote machine is as follows:

pscp *user@hostname:remote-filename local-filename*

where `user` is the user ID to which you will connect on the remote machine, `hostname` is the hostname or IP address of the remote machine, `remote-filename` is the full path and name of the file on the remote machine to download and `local-filename` is the full path and name of the downloaded file.

It is not necessary to specify the directory for the `remote-filename` or `target-filename` arguments. If the directory is not specified in the `remote-filename` argument, PSCP assumes the file is in the remote home directory of the user ID that is specified. If the directory is not specified in the `local-filename` argument, PSCP will download the file into the current directory. However, both arguments are required, so if you do not wish to change the name of the downloaded file and you want to put it into the current local directory, specify "." for the `local-filename` argument. "." represents the current directory:

- Here is an example of a user using PSCP to connect to machine server.example.com as user sshuser and downloading the file named test.pl to the current directory:

```
C:\>pscp sshuser@server.example.com:test.pl .
sshuser@server.example.com's password: ********
test.pl        |     0 kB |   0.1 kB/s | ETA: 00:00:00 | 100%

C:\>
```

The syntax for uploading a file is as follows:

pscp *local-filename user@hostname:remote-filename*

where `user` is the user to connect to on the remote machine, `hostname` is the hostname or IP address of the remote machine, `local-filename` is the full path and name of the local file to upload and `remote-filename` is the full path and name of the remote uploaded file. If no directory is specified for the `local-filename` argument, the current local directory will be used. If no directory is specified for the `remote-filename` argument, the remote home directory of the user logging in will be used. However, the colon following the hostname must still be present.

- Here is an example of a user using PSCP to connect to machine `server.example.com` as user `sshuser` and uploading all files named `test.*` to `/tmp`:

```
C:\>pscp test.* sshuser@server.example.com:/tmp
sshuser@server.example.com's password:
test.c         |     0 kB |   0.1 kB/s | ETA: 00:00:00 | 100%
test.sh        |     0 kB |   0.2 kB/s | ETA: 00:00:00 | 100%

C:\>
```

Section 4 - Using Public Key Authentication

Problem: Normally when you start an SSH session you will authenticate to the remote server using a password. This may pose a security problem in that if anyone were able to discover your password, they would be able to log in and impersonate you. To alleviate this problem, public key authentication can be used.

Step 4.1 Authentication with Public Keys

Public key authentication uses a key-pair, consisting of a public key and a private key, to authenticate to the remote server. The two keys are mathematically related such that anything encrypted with the public key can be decrypted only with the private key.

When public key authentication takes place, a number of steps occur. After the client contacts the server to log in, the server will encrypt a random message using the public key of the client and will send this encrypted message to the client. Using its private key, the client will decrypt the message, combine it with an identifier for the session, create an MD5 hash of the decrypted message and identifier, and send the MD5 hash back to the server. The server will create an MD5 hash of the random message and session identifier and compare it to the one it received from the client. If the hashes match, authentication is successful. This greatly reduces the likelihood that a man-in-the-middle attack can be used to intercept the login credentials. This is covered in more detail in section 5.2.7.

Of course, this method is not foolproof. If someone were to obtain the private key for a user, they could still log in and impersonate that user. Because of this, the private key is encrypted and protected with a passphrase. To unlock the private key and log in, the correct passphrase must be known. This adds a level of complexity to the authentication process, but makes the process more secure. Setting up this authentication requires a little bit of work.

Problem: SSH private keys are protected with a passphrase rather than a password. What makes a good passphrase?

Step 4.2 Passphrase Considerations

A passphrase differs from a password in that it should be composed of multiple words and more difficult to guess. The same rules that apply to creating good passwords also apply to creating good passphrases. The following is a list of suggestions for creating a good passphrase.

1. Make the passphrase at least 6 words or about 40 characters long. The longer the passphrase, the harder it will be to guess.

2. Use a mixture of upper- and lower-case letters within the passphrase.

3. Use non-alphabetic characters, such as numbers or punctuation, within the passphrase. The use of non-alphabetic characters makes a passphrase increasingly difficult to guess.

4. Don't make your passphrase a common or popular sentence or phrase. Using a string of nonsensical or random words will make your passphrase stronger.

Of course, it is possible to use an empty or null passphrase when using SSH. This is *strongly discouraged* as anyone who is able to obtain your private key would be able to impersonate you. However, there are times when an empty passphrase may be necessary, such as for an automated script or batch job. In these cases, it is recommended that a separate account on the remote machine be created for the automated script or batch job. By creating a separate account and limiting the account's privileges, you can at least minimize damage if it is compromised.

Problem: How can a key-pair be created in OpenSSH?

Step 4.3 How to Generate a Key Pair Using OpenSSH

Action 4.3.1 – Generating your public/private key-pair

The `ssh-keygen` command is utilized to generate your public and private keys. OpenSSH provides authentication methods via a choice of three public key "cryptosystems": RSA1, RSA, and DSA. RSA1 works with SSHv1 while RSA and DSA are for SSHv2. RSA and DSA use different techniques for authenticating and have different capabilities, but for purposes of this guide, either will suffice.

- To create a key-pair, run `ssh-keygen` with the `-t` option. The -t option specifies which cryptosystem you want the key to use. The valid options are "rsa", "dsa" or "rsa1". In this example, we have elected to use RSA authentication:
  ```
  $ ssh-keygen -t rsa
  Generating public/private rsa key pair
  ```

- Next you will be prompted for a passphrase, which is used to encrypt the private key. After you enter the passphrase you will be asked to verify it (See Step 4.2 for instructions on how to create a good passphrase.):
  ```
  Enter file in which to save the key (/home/sshuser/.ssh/id_rsa):
  Enter passphrase (empty for no passphrase): *********************
  Enter same passphrase again: *********************
  ```

- If the two passphrases do not match, you will be given an error message and asked to enter the passphrases in again, as shown below.
  ```
  Passphrases do not match.  Try again.
  Enter passphrase (empty for no passphrase): *********************
  Enter same passphrase again: *********************
  ```

- Once the passphrases match, ssh-keygen will display a message indicated where the public and private keys will be saved.
  ```
  Your identification has been saved in /home/sshuser/.ssh/id_rsa.
  Your public key has been saved in /home/sshuser/.ssh/id_rsa.pub.
  The key fingerprint is:
  9a:7a:87:33:14:d2:12:72:7c:3f:ea:54:a4:2e:b6:ba sshuser@server.example.com
  ```

It is important that you utilize a passphrase you will be able to recall but that would be difficult for someone else to guess. The passphrase is unrecoverable, so if you forget it, you will have to regenerate the public/private keys and a new passphrase.

If you suspect someone may know your passphrase, you should delete your old key pair and create a new one, using a different passphrase. You can also simply change your passphrase on the existing key, **but keep in mind this does not help if your key has already been compromised and someone has it in their possession.**

To generate a new passphrase on an existing key, use the `-p` parameter with `ssh-keygen`:
```
$ ssh-keygen -p
Enter file in which the key is (/home/sshuser/.ssh/id_rsa):
Enter old passphrase: *********************
Key has comment '/home/sshuser/.ssh/id_rsa'
Enter new passphrase (empty for no passphrase): *********************
Enter same passphrase again: *********************
Your identification has been saved with the new passphrase.
```

Your newly created public and private key files are stored within your default home directory under the sub-directory named `.ssh` (the `known-hosts` file was previously created in this directory when you first attempted a remote SSH connection):

```
$ cd $HOME
$ cd .ssh
$ ls -al
total 10
drwx------    2 sshuser    150         512 Feb 11 11:29 .
drwxr-xr-x   11 sshuser    150         512 Feb 11 10:58 ..
-rw-------    1 sshuser    150         736 Feb 11 11:29 id_rsa
-rw-r--r--    1 sshuser    150         603 Feb 11 11:29 id_rsa.pub
-rw-r--r--    1 sshuser    150         458 Dec 20 14:46 known_hosts
```

There are several other ssh-keygen options — please refer to the man page, for details:

```
$ man ssh-keygen
Reformatting page.   Please Wait... done

User Commands                                            SSH-KEYGEN(1)

NAME
     ssh-keygen - authentication key generation,  management  and
     conversion

SYNOPSIS
     ssh-keygen [-q] [-b bits] -t type   [-N  new_passphrase]  [-C
     comment] [-f output_keyfile]
     ssh-keygen -p [-P old_passphrase]   [-N  new_passphrase]  [-f
     keyfile]
     ssh-keygen -i [-f input_keyfile]
     ssh-keygen -e [-f input_keyfile]
     ssh-keygen -y [-f input_keyfile]
     ssh-keygen -c [-P passphrase] [-C comment] [-f keyfile]
     ssh-keygen -l [-f input_keyfile]
     ssh-keygen -B [-f input_keyfile]
     ssh-keygen -D reader
     ssh-keygen -U reader [-f input_keyfile]

DESCRIPTION
--More--(10%)
```

It should be noted that you can create and use more than one key-pair.

Action 4.3.2 – Configuring remote hosts to authenticate with your public key

Before your initial attempt to connect and authenticate using your key-pair and passphrase, you must configure the remote server to accept this form of communication. This is done by copying the contents of your public key file, $HOME/.ssh/id_rsa.pub (for RSA-style) to the respective authorized_keys file for each account to which you wish to login on the OpenSSH server. If you are using an early version of SSH version 2, the file may be called authorized_keys2.

For example, if the account "bob" on machine "client1" wants to connect to server "server1" as user "bob" via SSH and wants to be authenticated using a public key, then the public key contents for user "bob" on client1 ($HOME/.ssh/id_rsa.pub) will first have to be copied to the $HOME/.ssh/authorized_keys file for account "bob" on server1. If account "bob" on client1 wants to connect as account "ted" via SSH and using public key authentication on server1, then the public key contents must also be added to the HOME/.ssh/authorized_keys file for account "ted" as well.

How do you copy the public key information to the respective authorized_keys file(s)? There are a few methods, depending on whether an authorized_keys file already exists for that account. If you are performing a brand new setup of public key authentication and are sure that no authorized_keys files exists, then you can use any of a number of file copy methods — the sftp or scp commands documented previously would be recommended. Keep in mind that since you are just now configuring public key authentication, you will be using the UNIX password style of authentication to copy the public key information over. You can also use FTP or rcp, but keep in mind that those commands transfer all information in clear-text.

In the following example, user sshuser on OpenSSH client client.example.com uses sftp to transfer his public key to the authorized_keys file for user sshuser on OpenSSH server server.example.com (in this case, there is no existing authorized_keys file:)

```
$ pwd
/home/sshuser/.ssh
$ ls
id_dsa       id_dsa.pub    id_rsa       id_rsa.pub    known_hosts
$ sftp server.example.com
Connecting to server.example.com...
sshuser@server.example.com's password: *******
sftp> pwd
Remote working directory: /home/sshuser
sftp> cd .ssh
sftp> put id_rsa.pub authorized_keys
Uploading id_rsa.pub to /home/sshuser/.ssh/authorized_keys
sftp> bye
```

If the authorized_keys file already exists on the server, then you must be careful not to overwrite its contents - otherwise you might affect other OpenSSH clients trying to connect to this account. In this case, you would want to use copy-and-paste functions to *append* your public key information to the existing authorized_keys file. Be careful when using copy-and-paste functionality that you do not introduce additional line-end characters within the public key -- the public key must be one continuous line. As an alternative to copy-and-paste, the client could sftp the public key file to the OpenSSH server, then login to the server and append this file to the existing authorized_keys file.

For example, let's assume that the `authorized_keys` file for user `sshuser` on OpenSSH server `server.example.com` exists. User `sshuser` on OpenSSH client `client.example.com` wishes to add his public key to the existing file. Let's also assume that this information has been sent to the file `$HOME/.ssh/id_rsa.pub.copy` on `server.example.com` via sftp. In order to append the new public key information into the existing `authorized_keys` file we could use the following commands as user `sshuser` on server `server.example.com`:

```
$ cat $HOME/.ssh/id_rsa.pub.copy >>$HOME/.ssh/authorized_keys
```

Finally, it is extremely important that permissions for the `authorized_keys` file and its parent directory are set properly - otherwise the OpenSSH server will not honor public key authentication. The files in ~/.ssh, the .ssh directory, and the home directory must not be writable by any user other than the owner.

```
$ pwd
/home/sshuser/.ssh
$ ls -ld
drwxr-xr-x    8 sshuser    admin           512 Feb 12 17:09 .
$ ls -l
total 6
-rw-r--r--    1 sshuser    admin           446 Feb 12 17:11 authorized_keys
-rw-r--r--    1 sshuser    admin           688 Dec 20 14:57 known_hosts
-rw-------    1 sshuser    admin          1024 Feb 11 15:26 prng_seed
```

Action 4.3.3 – Using your public key for authentication to a remote server

Once the keys have been generated and your public key has been transferred to each server, you're ready to connect. OpenSSH is designed to detect public key authentication if it has been configured, so all you need to do is issue the appropriate SSH command to be authenticated and connect.

In the following example, OpenSSH client `client.example.com` is attempting to connect to OpenSSH server `server.example.com` with slogin. (`slogin` is actually just a symbolic link to `ssh`):

```
$ slogin server.example.com
Enter passphrase for key '/home/sshuser/.ssh/id_rsa': ***********************************************************
Last login: Wed Feb 12 17:09:25 2003 from client.example.com
$
```

Notice that instead of a "password" prompt, the user is now prompted for the "passphrase" associated with the public key -- this indicates that the server has recognized a new public key in the `authorized_keys` file. The server will give priority to the public key authentication before trying the UNIX password authentication method. If you get a "<user>@<server>'s `password`:" prompt instead of the "passphrase" prompt, then something is not configured correctly. A few things to double-check:

- Compare the user's public key file (`$HOME/.ssh/id_pub.rsa` on client) contents with the `authorized_keys` file on the server (`$HOME/.ssh/authorized_keys`). The public key must be identical in both locations. Make sure the public key is one continuous line with no embedded new-line characters.

- If you are connecting to a different user name on the server, remember to update the correct `authorized_keys` file. For example, if user "bob" on the client is connecting to user "ted" on the server, then the `$HOME/.ssh/id_pub.rsa` contents for user "bob" must exist in the `authorized_keys` for user "ted" on the server (`$HOME/.ssh/authorized_keys`).

- Check the permissions of the `authorized_keys` file and its parent directory. Remember this file must be writable by the owner only -- any write permissions granted to "group" or "other" will cause the public key authentication to fail.

Once you have the public key authentication configured and working, it will continue to be the first authentication method attempted for any of the OpenSSH client commands: `ssh`, `slogin`, `sftp`, `scp`, etc. If you forget your passphrase, all is not lost since **by default** OpenSSH will give you the opportunity to connect via the Unix password if the public key passphrase provided is wrong. For example:

```
$ ssh server.example.com
Enter passphrase for key ' /home/sshuser/.ssh/id_rsa':  ********************************
sshuser@server.example.com's password:  ********
Last login: Thu Feb 13 09:45:40 2003 from client.example.com
```

In this example, an incorrect passphrase was entered, so as the second method of authentication, OpenSSH prompted for the UNIX password. Again, this is the default out-of-the-box behavior for OpenSSH authentication - if you wish to enforce public key style authentication only, the sshd server's default configuration will need to be modified (see Tech Tip on this page). Keep in mind that in order to use the public key authentication again, you'll either need to recall the passphrase or generate new public/private keys and a new passphrase.

> **Tech Tip**
> Of course, allowing a secondary authentication can be considered as defeating the purpose of improved security, so don't be surprised if you are not given the opportunity to connect using a password. If this is the case, the administrator of the OpenSSH server has most likely set "PasswordAuthentication no" in the OpenSSH server's configuration file.

If for some reason you wish to temporarily use another authentication method, each of the SSH connection commands can also be invoked with the "-o" option to temporarily override public key authentication. For example:

```
$ ssh -o PreferredAuthentications=password server.example.com
sshuser@server.example.com's password:  ********
Last login: Thu Feb 13 10:42:35 2003 from client.example.com
$
```

Action 4.3.4 – Removing your public/private keys

There is no OpenSSH-specific command for removing your public and private keys. To remove them permanently, use the UNIX `rm` command. In the following example, the keys generated in Action 4.3.1 are removed:

```
$ cd $HOME/.ssh
$ ls -l
total 6
-rw-------    1 sshuser    150           951 Apr 10 11:19 id_rsa
-rw-r--r--    1 sshuser    150           223 Apr 10 11:19 id_rsa.pub
-rw-r--r--    1 sshuser    150           565 Feb 26 10:01 known_hosts
$ rm ./id_rsa ./id_rsa.pub
$
```

If you wish for just a temporary removal / disabling of your keys, then just rename the id files slightly and then change them back to their original names at the appropriate time.

Of course, you will also want to have your public key removed from any authorized_keys files to which it had earlier been added.

Problem: How do you generate a key pair using PuTTY?

Step 4.4 How to Generate a Key Using PuTTY

Action 4.4.1 – Generating a public / private key pair with PuTTY

PuTTY comes with the program PuTTYgen to generate public and private key pairs. To use PuTTYgen:

- Double-click on the desktop icon created for PuTTYgen or select it from the **Start Menu** to execute the program.
- The window that appears contains three sections: **Key**, **Actions** and **Parameters**. Since we do not have a key pair yet, we need to generate one. However, we first need to decide on which parameters to supply.

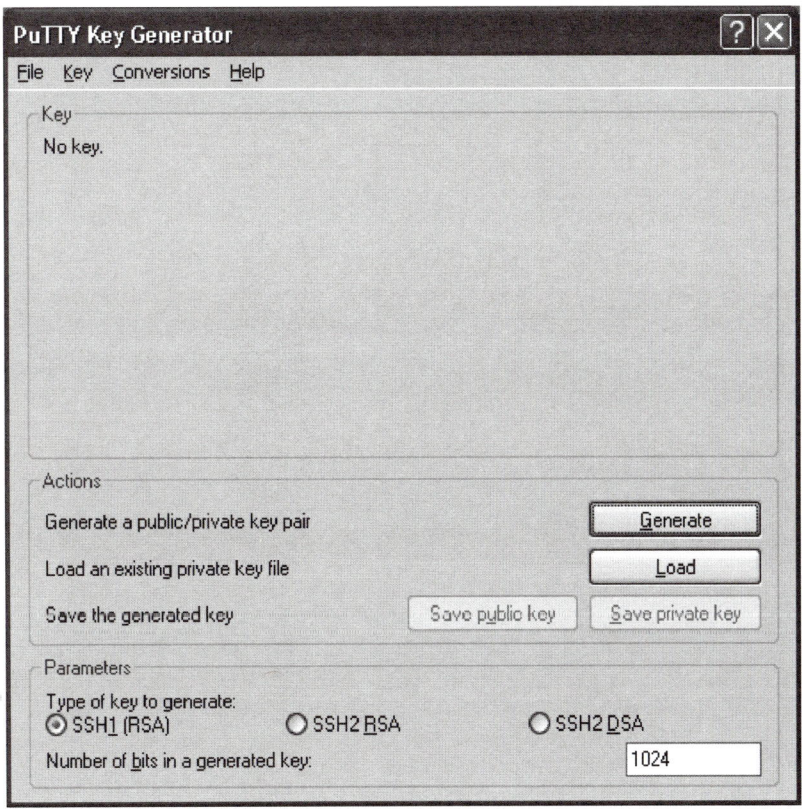

In the **Parameters** section are three options for the type of key to generate. SSHv1 only supports one type of key, so if you need to authenticate to a server that only supports SSHv1 make sure the radio button next to SSH1 (RSA) is selected.

If you will be connecting to a server that supports SSHv2, you have two choices for keys: SSH2 RSA and SSH2 DSA. The server you are connecting to may only allow one type of key, so you may have no choice as to what type of key you need to create. Click on the radio button next to the type of key you choose to create.

- Select the length of the key. The default length for a key within PuTTYgen is 1024 bits, which should be sufficient. Unless you need to change the length for specific reasons, leave 1024 in the **Number of bits in a generated key** field.
- Once both the key type and length are selected, click on the **Generate** button in the **Actions** section.
- PuTTYgen will now ask you to create some randomness by moving your mouse around the blank area of the program window. Move your mouse around until the progress bar fills completely.

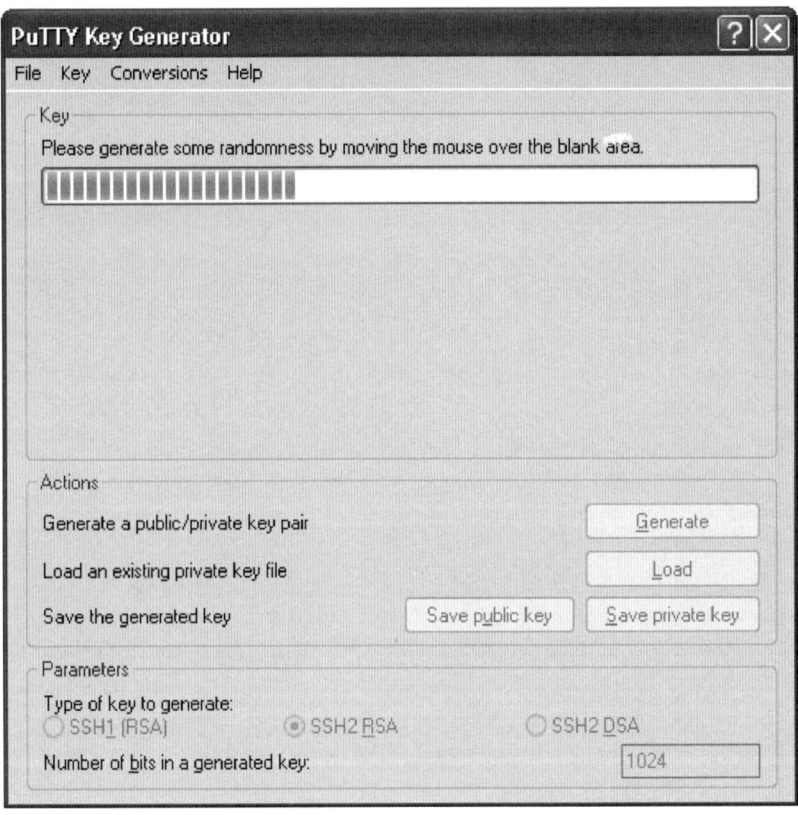

- When the progress bar has filled completely, it will be reset and PuTTYgen will begin to create your key. Once the progress bar has filled once again, the key will have been created and a new window will appear.

HOW TO GENERATE A KEY USING PuTTY

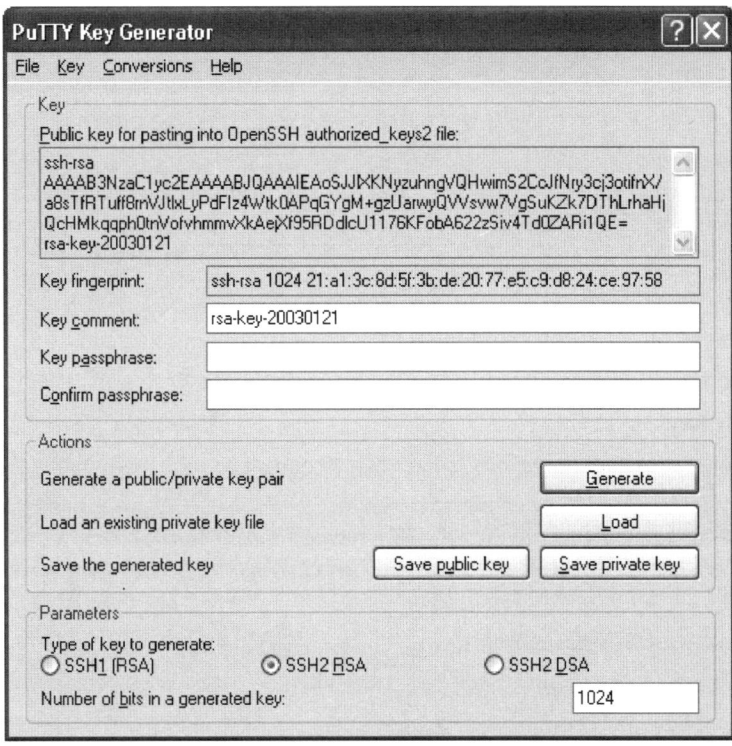

- The new window has a number of fields that you should fill in before saving the public and private key. The first is the **Key Comment** field.

  The **Key Comment** field allows you to add a comment to help you remember the purpose of this key-pair. This comment will be displayed whenever PuTTY asks you for the passphrase to unlock the key. A comment is not required, so it can be left blank.

- The next field is the **Key Passphrase** field. This is the phrase for which you will be prompted whenever you try to connect to a remote system. There are no minimum requirements for creating the passphrase and in fact it can be blank. A good passphrase, however, should be at least 6 words in length with random case and punctuation. See step 4.2 for more information on creating a good passphrase.

  As you enter a passphrase into the **Key Passphrase** field, you will not be able to see what you are typing as asterisks or bars will appear to prevent anyone from "shoulder surfing" and seeing your passphrase.

> **NOTE:** *You may be tempted to leave your passphrase blank. Don't! While there are times when this may be necessary, generally you should never have a blank passphrase for your personal account. If you left the passphrase blank and someone were able to get your private key, they would be able to authenticate to the remote server as you without authentication. The only time you should use a blank passphrase is when you need to run scripts automatically using SSH. When this happens, you should create and lock down a separate account on the remote server to minimize the potential damage if the account were compromised.*

- Retype the passphrase in the **Confirm passphrase** field. This is to avoid potential typographical errors.

> **NOTE: Make sure your passphrase is obscure but memorable as there is no way to recover it!**

- Next, click on the **Save private key** button in the **Actions** section to save your private key to disk. If the passphrases you typed do not match, an error will appear.
- If your passphrase fields match, a dialog box will appear asking you where on disk to save the private key. The directory into which you choose to save the private key should be appropriately protected, to keep your private key as secure as possible. You could even keep it safe on a floppy disk, as long as the floppy disk is secured.
- Type in a filename for the key in the **File name** field.
- The **Save as type** field should display **PuTTY Private Key** Files. If it does not, select it from the drop down list.
- Click on the **Save** button. If the save is successful, you will be returned back to the PuTTYgen screen.
- Now you need to save your public key. Click on the button named **Save public key**.
- This will open a dialog box similar to the one that was used to save the private key. In the dialog box, select the directory to which you want the public key saved.
- Once the destination directory for the public key has been selected, type the filename for the key into the **File name** field. The drop down box for the **Save as type** will display **All files**. This is fine, as the public key will be saved as a normal text file that you can copy as needed. You may wish to consider using a ".pub" extension for the public key.
- Click on the **Save** button. If the save is successful, you will be returned back to the PuTTYgen screen.

Action 4.4.2 – Setting up public key authentication
Now that your public and private keys are created, you need to set up the remote server to accept our newly generated keys:

- Leaving PuTTYgen open, launch PuTTY and open up a connection to the server with which you wish to use public key authentication. Enter your authentication information when prompted to log in to the server.
- After receiving a prompt, enter `cd .ssh`. This will place you into the directory where you will store your public key.
- Look at the listing for the directory by typing `ls -l`. The name of the file you are looking for will depend on the version of OpenSSH you are using. If you are using SSHv1 or SSHv2, you want to find a file called `authorized_keys`. If you are using an early version of SSHv2, the file may be named `authorized_keys2`.

```
login as: sshuser
sshuser@server.example.com's password: *******

[sshuser@server.example.com]$ cd .ssh
[sshuser@server.example.com]$ ls -l
total 2
-rw-rw-r--   1 sshuser   sshuser   226 Aug 11 12:46 authorized_keys
-rw-r--r--   1 sshuser   sshuser   223 Aug 10 13:27 known_hosts

[sshuser@server.example.com]$
```

If the file does not exist, you can create it with your favorite editor.
(In the rest of this example, we will refer to this file as the `authorized_keys` file, although the actual filename may differ depending on your version of SSH.)

- At the command prompt of the remote machine, use your favorite editor to open or create the `authorized_keys` file.

- Switch back to PuTTYgen on your Windows desktop. In the **Key** section, there is a window entitled **Public key for pasting into OpenSSH authorized_keys2 file:**. Highlight all of the text within that window and copy it into the Windows buffer by pressing Control+C.

- Switch back to your SSH session with the `authorized_keys` file loaded in your favorite editor. Paste your public key into the file by pressing Control+V or Shift+Insert. Your public key should be pasted into the file as one continuous line (although the text will probably wrap). Save the file and exit your editor. If the `authorized_keys` file did not previously exist, make sure that the file is saved with the appropriate name, depending on your version of SSH.

- We now need to set the correct owner and permissions on the `authorized_keys` file. Run `ls -l` again at the command prompt to review the owner and permissions of the `authorized_keys` file.

> **NOTE: If the** `authorized_keys` **file does not have the correct owner or permissions, your SSH server may not allow you to log in using public key authentication.**

```
[sshuser@server.example.com]$ ls -l
total 2
-rw-rw-r--    1 sshuser   sshuser       238 Jan 21 22:20 authorized_keys
-rw-r--r--    1 sshuser   sshuser       223 Aug 10 13:27 known_hosts
[sshuser@server.example.com]$
```

- The user ID of the user you are trying to log in as should own the file (the owner is the third column in the `ls -l` listing). If it is not, change ownership now using the `chown` command as shown below.
    ```
    [sshuser@server.example.com]$ chown sshuser authorized_keys
    ```

- The file permissions are the first column of the `ls -l` listing. The file should be readable by everyone but only writable only by the owner of the file. The correct permissions should be as follows:
    ```
    -rw-r--r--    1 sshuser   sshuser       238 Jan 21 22:20 authorized_keys
    ```

If the `authorized_keys` file permissions are incorrect, change them with the `chmod` command, as shown below:
```
[sshuser@server.example.com]$ chmod 644 authorized_keys
```

Action 4.4.3 – Using PuTTY to log in with public key authentication
Now we need to tell PuTTY to use public key authentication to log into the server:

- Double-click on the icon that was created for PuTTY or select it from the to start another instance of PuTTY.

- In the **Session** category of the PuTTY configuration screen, enter the host name or IP address of the server that you've configured for public key authentication.

- Make sure the SSH protocol is selected by clicking on the radio button next to **SSH** in the **Protocol** section.

- In the left-hand window, select the **Connection->SSH->Auth** category. This is the category that controls some of the options for SSH authentication:

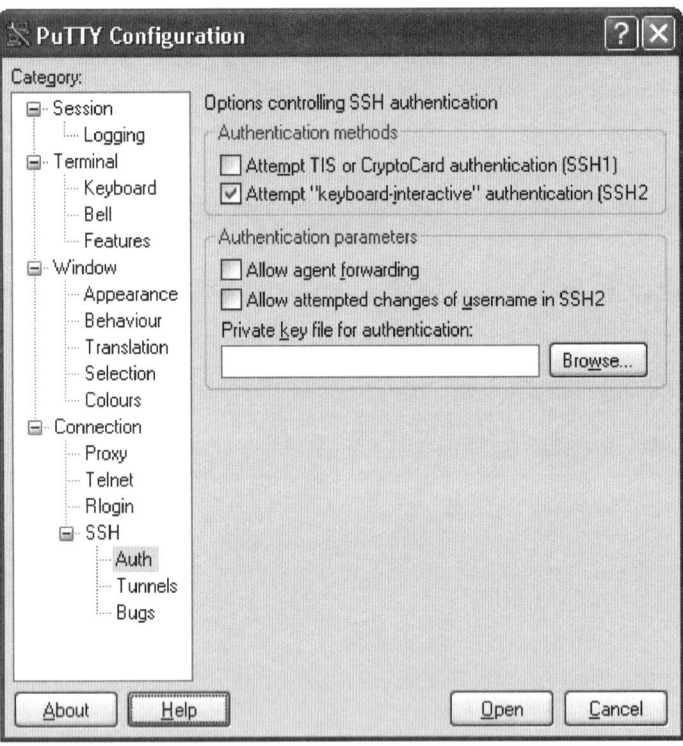

- In the section marked **Authentication parameters**, click on the **Browse** button located below the field entitled **Private key file for authentication:**.

- Click on the **Browse** button and a dialog box will appear allowing you to specify the private key file you created for your connection to the server. Once you have selected the private key file, click on the **Open** button and you will return to the PuTTY configuration screen. The name of the file in which the private key is stored should now be listed in the **Private key file for authentication:** field.

- Click on the **Open** button. PuTTY will now attempt to contact the remote server and authenticate using public key authentication.

- Next, PuTTY will ask for your user name. This is the user name of the account on the remote host.

- If public key authentication has been configured correctly, you will be told that you are authenticating with your public key and you will be asked for the passphrase for your key.
  ```
  login as: sshuser
  Authenticating with public key sshuser@server.example.com
  Passphrase for key "sshuser@server.example.com": ***************************
  [sshuser@server.example.com]$
  ```

- If the passphrase was not entered correctly, you will be given 2 more attempts to try again. After the 3rd attempt, the SSH connection will either abort, or, if the OpenSSH server has been configured to allow both public key AND password authentication, you will be prompted for the account password.

Action 4.4.4 – Use public key authentication from the command line PuTTY tools

We have seen that we can use public key authentication with PuTTY, the graphical SSH interface, but sometimes we may want to use public key authentication when using the PuTTY command line tools PSCP, PSFTP and Plink.

Each of these programs provides a `-i` command line option for specifying the path and filename of the file containing the private key. Whenever the `-i` option is specified for any of these tools, they will automatically try to authenticate using public key authentication.

The following example shows how to use PSCP to transfer files using public key authentication. The same procedure is used for PSFTP and Plink:

- Open a Windows command prompt by clicking on the **Start Menu** and selecting **Run**. In the Open prompt, type `cmd` if you are running Windows NT/2000/XP or `command` if you are running Windows 9x/ME and press the **OK** button.
- At the Windows command prompt, use PSCP to copy a file using the -i option with the path and file name of the file containing the private key, as shown below:

```
C:\temp>pscp -i "c:\temp\mykeys\my_private.PPK" test.pl sshuser@server.example.com:.
Authenticating with public key sshuser@server.example.com
Passphrase for key "sshuser@server.example.com": *************************

test.pl          |           22 kB |   22.0 kB/s | ETA: 00:00:00 | 100%
C:\temp>
```

Action 4.4.5 – Removing your public/private keys

Since your public and private keys are stored locally in a file, removing them is as simple as deleting the file. Of course, this will only delete them on your local machine and not any servers where you may have copied your public key. To remove those, refer to Action 4.3.4.

Problem: Using public key authentication makes logging in to a server with SSH more secure, but less convenient due to having to type in a longer and more complex passphrase.

Step 4.5 How to use OpenSSH Passphrase Agents

Action 4.5.1 – Use ssh-agent and ssh-add to store your private keys in memory

To make public key authentication more convenient to use, the OpenSSH developers created the ssh-agent and ssh-add programs. These programs are designed to keep your private keys decrypted in memory for your *current* session. With ssh-agent, you will not need to type a passphrase when connecting to a remote system, since the private key resides in memory.

While this makes using public key authentication more convenient, it should be noted that it does pose a small security risk as your private key is sitting in memory decrypted. If a rogue program were able to read that portion of memory, it would be able to use the private key and log in to the remote server using your credentials.

ssh-agent can be run in one of two ways. The first way is to enter `eval ``ssh-agent``` at the command line, which runs ssh-agent in the background and sets two environment variables for its use, SSH_AUTH_SOCK and SSH_AGENT_PID.

```
[sshuser@server.example.com]$ eval `ssh-agent`
Agent pid 19401
[sshuser@server.example.com]$ echo $SSH_AGENT_PID
19401
[sshuser@server.example.com]$ echo $SSH_AUTH_SOCK
/tmp/ssh-XXZCgt5e/agent.19401
[sshuser@server.example.com]$
```

The second way to run ssh-agent is to supply a program name - typically a shell – as a command line option. When you run ssh-agent this way, that program will be run with SSH_AUTH_SOCK and SSH_AGENT_PID already set.

```
[sshuser@server.example.com]$ ssh-agent /bin/bash
[sshuser@server.example.com]$ echo $SSH_AGENT_PID
1272
[sshuser@server.example.com]$ echo $SSH_AUTH_SOCK
/tmp/ssh-XXZCgt5e/agent.1271
[sshuser@server.example.com]$
```

- Once ssh-agent has started up successfully, you need to add the private keys into memory. This is done using the ssh-add program as follows:

```
[sshuser@server.example.com]$ ssh-add
Enter passphrase for /home/sshuser/.ssh/id_rsa:
Identity added: /home/sshuser/.ssh/id_rsa (/home/sshuser/.ssh/id_rsa)
[sshuser@server.example.com]$
```

When given no arguments, the ssh-add program looks for the files `.ssh/id_rsa`, `.ssh/id_dsa` and `.ssh/identity` in the home directory of the user and adds the private keys in these files into memory.

Alternatively, ssh-add accepts a filename as an argument. The filename specified is expected to contain the private-keys which ssh-add will load into memory.

If a private key requires a passphrase to decrypt it, ssh-add will prompt the user for the passphrase. If the passphrase is entered correctly, the private key will be stored in memory.

Action 4.5.2 – Verify the private keys are in memory

Once the private keys have been loaded into memory, it may be helpful to verify that they are really there. This can be done using the `-l` option. This option will display all private keys that are currently in memory:

```
[sshuser@server.example.com]$ ssh-add -l
1024 5b:62:e3:14:80:72:e0:58:03:36:29:52:29:90:a9:04 /home/sshuser/.ssh/id_rsa (RSA)
[sshuser@server.example.com]$
```

Action 4.5.3 – Using ssh-agent to automatically log in to a remote machine

Now that the private keys are loaded into memory, subsequent SSH authentications will be handled automatically by ssh-agent, assuming the correct keys have been loaded. ssh-agent will perform the authentication proxy for any OpenSSH program, including scp and sftp.

In the following example, `sshuser` is attempting to create an SSH session to remote host `server.example.com` from `client.example.com`. Public key authentication is used and normally `sshuser` would have to enter the passphrase associated with the private key to authenticate, but since ssh-agent has the private key decrypted and loaded into memory, sshuser is not prompted for authentication:

```
[sshuser@client.example.com]$ ssh server.example.com
[sshuser@server.example.com]$
```

Action 4.5.4 – Removing private keys from memory

The ssh-add program can accept the `-d` or `-D` options to remove private keys from memory. The `-D` option will cause ALL private keys currently in memory to be removed. The `-d` option has the same effect if no arguments are supplied to it. However, if a filename associated with a private key in memory is provided with the -d option, only that private key will be removed from memory.

Action 4.5.5 – Shutting down ssh-agent

SSH-agent can be shut down via a number of ways, depending on how it was started up.

If ssh-agent was started using `eval ``ssh-agent```, it should be shut down using `eval` with the `-k` option as shown below:

```
[sshuser@server.example.com]$ eval `ssh-agent -k`
Agent pid 19401 killed
```

Shutting ssh-agent down this way will shut down the running instance of ssh-agent and also unset the environment variables that were set.

> **Note:** *If ssh-agent was started with the eval command, it must be shut down manually before you log out or it will remain memory-resident and active. If ssh-agent is used frequently, it may be a good idea to add eval `ssh-agent –k` to the appropriate logout script for your shell.*

If ssh-agent was started with a program passed as a parameter, it will shut down when that program terminates. For example, if you supplied a shell name to ssh-agent as a command line argument, ssh-agent will terminate when you log out of the shell.

Step 4.6 How to use PuTTY Passphrase Agents

Action 4.6.1 – Use Pageant to store your private keys in memory

To make public key authentication more convenient, the developers of PuTTY created Pageant.

Pageant is a program included with PuTTY that will keep your decrypted private keys in memory so you only have to enter your passphrase once rather than every time you authenticate to a server using public key authentication.

While this will make your day-to-day use more convenient, please keep in mind that it also poses a slight risk, since other applications (including viruses) might be able to access these decrypted keys in memory.

To use Pageant:

- Start Pageant by selecting it from the **Start Menu**. No windows will open, but the icon for Pageant will display in the system tray, as show below. Pageant's icon is the computer wearing the hat.

- Next, we need to load our private key into Pageant. Right click on the icon for Pageant in the system tray. A menu with a number of options will appear. Select **Add Key**.
- A dialog box will open and ask you to find and select the file containing the private key you wish to load. After you select the file, click the **Open** button.

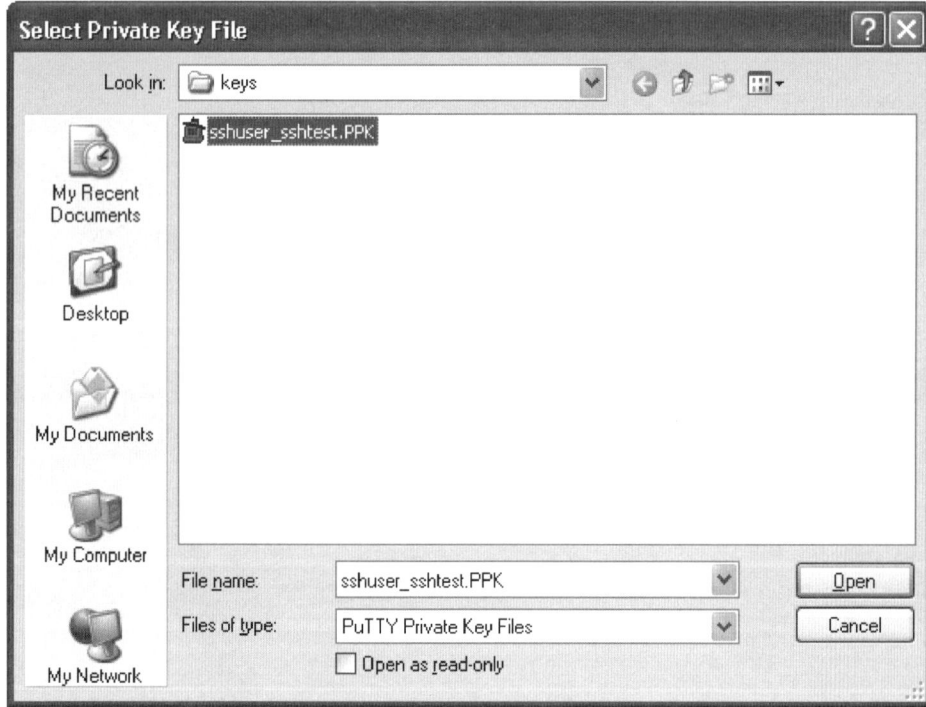

- Next you will be prompted for the passphrase to unlock this key. Enter the passphrase and click on the **OK** button.

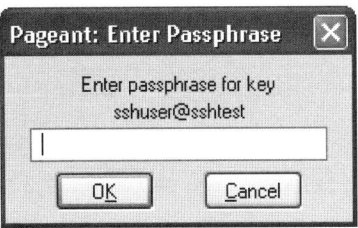

If the passphrase you entered was incorrect, you will be re-prompted.

Action 4.6.2 – Verify Pageant has your private key stored
Now we should verify that the key is loaded into Pageant:

- Right click on the icon for Pageant in the system tray and select **View Keys**.
- A window titled **Pageant Key List** will open. This window lists all of the keys currently loaded into Pageant. From this window you can also add new keys or remove keys previously loaded.

You should see the key that you loaded into Pageant listed in this window. If not, you should attempt to load your key into Pageant again.

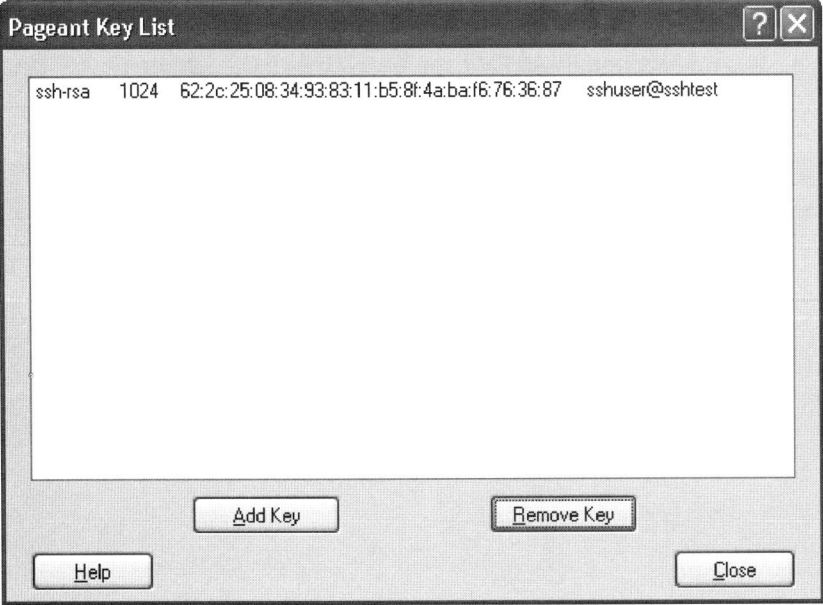

Action 4.6.3 – Using Pageant to automatically log in to a remote machine

Now that we have verified that our key is loaded into Pageant, we can attempt to log in to a remote machine automatically:

- Launch a new instance of PuTTY. With Pageant running, this can be done in a few different ways. First, you can open PuTTY by double clicking on the icon for PuTTY or by selecting it from the **Start Menu**.

  Second, if you have a session already saved for the server to which you wish to connect, you can right click on the icon for Pageant located in the system tray. There is an option in the menu labeled **Saved Sessions** which will open up to a listing of all your saved sessions. You can select the desired session from that listing and PuTTY will open and try to connect to the remote server you selected.

  Finally, if you do not have a session already saved, you can right click on the icon for Pageant in the system tray and select **New Session** from the menu. This will launch PuTTY into the configuration screen.

- If you are not using a saved session, enter all information needed to connect to the remote server in the PuTTY configuration screen. You do not have to select a private key. After you have entered all required information, click on the **Open** button.

- PuTTY will now attempt to connect to the remote server. If it is successful, it will ask you for the user ID to log in under as shown below:
  ```
  login as: sshuser
  ```

- After you enter the user ID, you should receive a message that you are authenticating with your public key as shown below:
  ```
  Authenticating with public key "sshuser@example.com" from agent
  Last login: Wed Jan 22 11:20:43 2003 from 192.168.1.10
  [sshuser@server.example.com]$
  ```

  When you were logging in to the remote server, PuTTY saw that Pageant was running and asked Pageant for the key to the remote server. Since the key for the remote server was loaded into Pageant and had already been decrypted, PuTTY was able to use the key to log in to the remote server.

Action 4.6.4 – Using Pageant with command line tools

If Pageant is already running in the background, the command line tools that come with PuTTY will automatically detect this and will authenticate with Pageant. An example of PSCP copying a file to a remote server is shown below. The -v verbose option has been added to see PSCP communicate with Pageant:

```
C:\>pscp -v test.txt sshuser@server.example.com:.
Looking up host "server.example.com"
Connecting to 192.168.1.10 port 22
Server version: SSH-2.0-OpenSSH_3.1p1
We believe remote version has SSH2 RSA padding bug
We claim version: SSH-2.0-PuTTY-Release-0.53b
Using SSH protocol version 2
Doing Diffie-Hellman group exchange
Doing Diffie-Hellman key exchange
Host key fingerprint is:
ssh-rsa 1024 41:61:b5:ab:c5:c5:01:46:ac:ef:a1:28:54:c0:1c:53
Using username "sshuser".
Pageant is running. Requesting keys.
```

```
Pageant has 1 SSH2 keys
Trying Pageant key #0
Authenticating with public key "sshuser@server.example.com" from agent
Sending Pageant's response
Access granted
Opened channel for session
Started a shell/command
Connected to server.example.com

Sending file test.txt, size=1477
test.txt           |          1 kB |    1.4 kB/s | ETA: 00:00:00 | 100%
Sent EOF message
Server sent command exit status 0

C:\>
```

Problem: Automated scripts and file transfers cannot decrypt password-protected public keys.

Step 4.7 Using Public Key Authentication for Automated File Transfers

It is possible to use public key authentication to automatically transfer files from one machine to another. While this is usually not recommended, it may be desirable for batch scripts. However, this involves setting a blank passphrase which clearly leads to some risks. Therefore this mechanism should only be used for a one-way connection between two specific, non-privileged user IDs on different hosts.

Action 4.7.1 – Decide who trusts who

- Decide which system trusts which and what user ids are going to be used on each. Minimal privilege (non-root, not-a-real-person) user ids are best for system-to-system trust relationships. In general, the less secure, less vital system should trust the more secure, more critical system.

    In the example below, we will set up `sshuser` on `client.example.com` to connect to `server.example.com` as user `sshuser2`.

Action 4.7.2 – Generate a key pair

- First, a key pair needs to be generated for `sshuser` on `server.example.com`. Generating a key pair is detailed in step 4.3 of this book. However, when a key pair is generated for an automated transfer, it should be configured so that we are never prompted to decrypt the private key.

To accomplish this, do not enter a passphrase when prompted by the `ssh-keygen` program - instead just press `enter`. This can also be accomplished by supplying the `-P` option with a null passphrase to `ssh-keygen` (e.g. `-P " "`). When you do not enter a passphrase, `ssh-keygen` understand this to indicate that you do not want the private key encrypted:

```
[sshuser@client.example.com]$ ssh-keygen -t rsa
Generating public/private rsa key pair.
Enter file in which to save the key (/home/sshuser/.ssh/id_rsa):
Enter passphrase (empty for no passphrase):
Enter same passphrase again:
Your identification has been saved in /home/sshuser/.ssh/id_rsa.
Your public key has been saved in /home/sshuser/.ssh/id_rsa.pub.
The key fingerprint is:
7e:ab:80:12:06:0f:b9:1f:f1:64:b0:0a:00:7c:69:b4 sshuser@client.example.com
[sshuser@client.example.com]$
```

- Keep in mind that since the private key is now stored unencrypted, if anyone were able to get the private key file, they would be able to log in on the remote machine without an authentication challenge. This is the reason we use a restricted user account on both machines when creating key pairs with no passphrase.

Action 4.7.3 – Copy the public key to the remote system

- The key pair for `sshuser` should now be created and stored in the `~sshuser/.ssh` directory, where `~sshuser` is sshuser's home directory, in either the `id_dsa.pub` or `id_rsa.pub` file, depending on which type of key pair you created:

```
[sshuser@client.example.com]$ cd .ssh
[sshuser@client.example.com]$ ls -l
total 7
-rw-r--r--    1 sshuser   sshuser    223 Jan 22 11:00 authorized_keys
-rw-------    1 sshuser   sshuser    883 Feb 24 12:29 id_rsa
-rw-r--r--    1 sshuser   sshuser    239 Feb 24 12:29 id_rsa.pub
-rw-r--r--    1 sshuser   sshuser   2880 Feb 21 08:50 known_hosts
[sshuser@client.example.com]$ cat id_rsa.pub
ssh-rsa
AAAAB3NzaC1yc2EAAAABIwAAAIEAvXDPUt6OScgSrCFcYffvMTRVK8+IzOe1JKGDoIwCK1ZB1E1GGkGQPHftVnan5oc+hX6C1wg66TFL
M/38jtQhWmGpLo00ZbfzmA9qrE72T/G58Vl57chZOmFWMWzXXYuni8v7ThT2pMXTY5csJRqX4pPquM76LGK6Qtpf5vyQH9M=
sshuser@client.example.com
[sshuser@client.example.com]$
```

- The public key of `sshuser` now needs to be copied over to `server.example.com` for `sshuser2` to use. This can be done any way that is convenient. Since we are transferring the public key and we don't care who sees the public key, it can be transferred in a clear-text manner, such as by email or FTP:

```
[sshuser@client.example.com]$ scp id_rsa.pub sshuser2@server.example.com:~
sshuser2@server.example.com's password: *******
id_rsa.pub        100% |*****************************|   239   00:00
```

- Once sshuser's public key is copied to server.example.com, open an SSH session to server.example.com and log in as sshuser2. If you have restricted sshuser2's account such that it is unable to log in, you will have to log in to server.example.com as root, and then become sshuser2 using the su command:

```
[sshuser@client.example.com]$ ssh sshuser2@server.example.com
sshuser2@server.example.com's password: *******
Last login: Mon Feb 24 11:19:15 2003 from client.example.com
[sshuser2@server.example.com]$
```

- Once you log in as sshuser2, change to the .ssh directory in sshuser2's home directory. You should see a file named authorized_keys.

```
[sshuser2@server.example.com]$ cd .ssh
[sshuser2@server.example.com]$ ls -l
total 12
-rw-r--r--  1  sshuser2   staff    227 Feb 24 12:21 authorized_keys
-rw-r--r--  1  sshuser2   staff    223 Dec  9 14:25 known_hosts
[sshuser2@server.example.com]$
```

- Append sshuser's public key, which you copied, to the authorized_keys file. Be careful when appending the key to the file as the key should remain as one continuous line (i.e. no carriage-returns or linefeeds).

```
[sshuser2@server.example.com]$ ls ~/id_rsa.pub
/home/sshuser2/id_rsa.pub
[sshuser2@server.example.com]$ cat ~/id_rsa.pub >> authorized_keys
[sshuser2@server.example.com]$ cat authorized_keys ssh-rsa
AAAAB3NzaC1yc2EAAAADJQAAAIEA2Rv612mkhAXokW2tvA/6w34OM2TzYS9xQmY9TQg07qMqp0UbQAuEQEUc7Oga6wY9jBBQWmLx7B3c
RuDdOQnASUugqQypuIVqqw4iaEi24qmrI6JTDCwEWZQ+ndODVXDDQeTVEVJLxNvvbwSvcvi3tV+7m26HooFYvoGWb7njJqk=
sshuser2@server.example.com
ssh-rsa
AAAAB3NzaC1yc2EAAAABIwAAAIEAvXDPUt60ScgSrCFcYffvMTRVK8+IzOe1JKGDoIwCKlZB1E1GGkGQPHftVnan5oc+hX6C1wg66TFL
M/38jtQhWmGpLo00ZbfzmA9qrE72T/G58Vl57chZOmFWMWzXXYuni8v7ThT2pMXTY5csJRqX4pPquM76LGK6Qtpf5vyQH9M=
sshuser@client.example.com
```

- Once sshuser's public key has been appended to the authorized_keys file successfully, you should be able to automatically log in and transfer files from client.example.com as user sshuser to server.example.com as sshuser2 without being prompted for authentication.

Action 4.7.4 – Verify that you are able to log in without an authentication prompt

In order to verify that the public key authentication is not prompting for a passphrase, try logging in from server.example.com as sshuser to server.example.com as sshuser2. If everything is configured properly, you should not be prompted for a passphrase and should log in automatically.

```
[sshuser@client.example.com]$ ssh sshuser2@server.example.com
Last login: Mon Feb 24 12:25:16 2003 from client.example.com
[sshuser2@server.example.com]$
```

Action 4.7.5 – Verify that a scp transfer works.

If you are able to log in to the remote system using OpenSSH without being prompted for a passphrase, you should be able to use scp to copy a file to `server.example.com` as `sshuser2` from `client.example.com` as `sshuser`, also with no passphrase:

```
[sshuser@client.example.com]$ scp test.pl sshuser2@server.example.com:~
test.pl      100% |*****************************|   151         00:00
[sshuser@client.example.com]$
```

Action 4.7.6 – Secure the connection

At this point you have created the capability for a user account on a client to log in to a server using public key authentication without being prompted for a passphrase. While this makes using public key authentication more convenient, it also opens up some security risks. Namely, the private key used to log in to the remote server is now sitting unencrypted. If a malicious attacker were able to obtain the unencrypted private key, he would be able to log in as the remote user. Therefore, some further restrictions should be put into place to lock down the use of the unencrypted private key.

OpenSSH provides a number of options that can be used to restrict a key used for authentication. These options are entered in the `authorized_keys` file on the remote server, immediately preceding the associated key entry. Multiple options can be used to further restrict the use of the key. The options available are described below.

- `from="hosts"` – The `from` option specifies IP addresses or resolvable hostnames that are allowed to use the key for authentication. Wildcards "*" and "?" and negation "!" can also be used to indicate which hosts are allowed to connect. Multiple hosts can be specified in a comma-delimited list. An example of a key using the `from` option is shown below:

```
from="192.168.1.10,*.example.com,!client.example.com" ssh-rsa AAAAB3NzaC1yc2Eaaaa253gAAIEAuG8ugce5+/
Cno2FCcyraJN2LK5Gsl+ujV8ad8s1lobh1donA20x6i9eNln8+LP76k2jMuLFtWEmc8MwmvrnIL2ZH2SOC90QpB3KwBuS6suVWT
X5AKkXpB5uEKMWQJjHoEFOQx7Kpzmkav83n73naE8u/oyagSIgLVxCIvEhk9XX8= sshuser@example.com
```

> **Note:** If the OpenSSH daemon is set to fall back to password authentication when public key authentication is not successful, a malicious user may still be able to log in to the system if they know the password for the account! That is because these options only restrict the use of the key, not the use of the account.

- `command="command"` – The `command` option specifies a command that is run immediately after the key is used for authentication. After the command executes, the SSH session will be terminated immediately. This option is extremely useful when you want to restrict the use of a key to single commands, such as backups or file copies.

```
command="/home/backup/backup.sh" ssh-rsa AAAAB3NzaC1yc2Eaaaa253gAAIEAuG8ugce5+/
Cno2FCcyraJN2LK5Gsl+ujV8ad8s1lobh1donA20x6i9eNln8+LP76k2jMuLFtWEmc8MwmvrnIL2ZH2SOC90QpB3KwBuS6suVWT
X5AKkXpB5uEKMWQJjHoEFOQx7Kpzmkav83n73naE8u/oyagSIgLVxCIvEhk9XX8= sshuser@example.com
```

- `environment="variable=value"` – The `environment` option specifies a variable that is added to the environment whenever the key is used. If this environment variable is already set, its previous value will be overwritten. This option can be useful for limiting the PATH environment variable in backup scripts to prevent certain attacks. This option can be specified multiple times.
  ```
  environment="PATH=/bin:/usr/bin",environment="TERM=vt100" ssh-rsa AAAAB3NzaC1yc2Eaaaa253gAAIEAuG8ugce5+/
  Cno2FCcyraJN2LK5Gsl+ujV8ad8s1lobhldonA20x6i9eNln8+LP76k2jMuLFtWEmc8MwmvrnIL2ZH2SOC90QpB3KwBuS6suVWT
  X5AKkXpB5uEKMWQJjHoEFOQx7Kpzmkav83n73naE8u/oyagSIgLVxCIvEhk9XX8= sshuser@example.com
  ```

- `permitopen="host:port"` – The `permitopen` option restricts local port forwarding to only the hosts and ports specified. Unlike the from option, wildcards and negation cannot be used. Multiple permitopen options can be specified. See step 6.1 for more information on port forwarding.
  ```
  permitopen="mail.example.com:25",permitopen="mail.example.com:143" ssh-rsa AAAAB3NzaC1yc2Eaaaa253gAAIE
  AuG8ugce5+/Cno2FCcyraJN2LK5Gsl+ujV8ad8s1lobhldonA20x6i9eNln8+LP76k2jMuLFtWEmc8MwmvrnIL2ZH2SOC90
  QpB3KwBuS6suVWTX5AKkXpB5uEKMWQJjHoEFOQx7Kpzmkav83n73naE8u/oyagSIgLVxCIvEhk9XX8= sshuser@example.com
  ```

- no-port-forwarding – This option will disallow any port forwarding when the key is used. See step 6.1 for more information on port forwarding.

- no-X11-forwarding – This option will disallow X11 forwarding when the key is used. See step 6.3 for more information on X11 forwarding.

- no-agent-forwarding – This option will disallow agent forwarding when the key is used. Agent forwarding is used in OpenSSH to allow your local OpenSSH daemon to contact an authentication agent (ssh-agent or Pageant) on a remote machine. Authentication agents are discussed in more detail in step 4.5.

- no-pty – This command prevents tty allocation to occur when the key is used. This is useful when you want a key to be used only for non-interactive commands, such as backups.
  ```
  no-pty,no-agent-forwarding,no-X11-forwarding,no-port-forwarding ssh-rsa AAAAB3NzaC1yc2Eaaaa253gAAIE
  AuG8ugce5+/Cno2FCcyraJN2LK5Gsl+ujV8ad8s1lobhldonA20x6i9eNln8+LP76k2jMuLFtWEmc8MwmvrnIL2ZH2SOC90
  QpB3KwBuS6suVWTX5AKkXpB5uEKMWQJjHoEFOQx7Kpzmkav83n73naE8u/oyagSIgLVxCIvEhk9XX8= sshuser@example.com
  ```

Section 5 - Troubleshooting SSH Connections

The primary purpose of this guide is to provide basic, step-by-step instructions for quickly installing, configuring, and using OpenSSH. Of course, as with most new ventures, you will most likely run into unexpected problems along the way. OpenSSH runs on numerous platforms so of course it would be an incredible, if not impossible, task to address all known problems encountered on every platform. This section was never intended to address every known problem but rather is intended to be a guide to help with general troubleshooting of SSH issues and also to address specific common problems.

You may have other troubleshooting techniques to share or may learn of solutions to new problems you encounter -- if you would like to share your findings, you are encouraged to do so via e-mail to **openssh@sans.org**.

Step 5.1 - General Troubleshooting

Action 5.1.1 - Verify download and installation/configuration of software

If you are encountering problems just getting OpenSSH to run, and/or are receiving error messages that indicate an install or configure problem, then of course the first place to start is to review the installation/configuration steps for the OpenSSH pre-requisite software and for OpenSSH itself (see Section I). Remember that certain software - such as Zlib and OpenSSL - must be installed **before** OpenSSH, since OpenSSH relies on them.

Before you get into specific install reviews, it's a good idea to make sure that you have a valid download file. It might appear obvious that you don't have a download problem if you were able to "unpack", install and compile the source code -- but stranger things have happened. Make sure that the size of the downloaded file (typically .tar, .Z, .gz, .zip) is equal to that provided (usually) by the download site. If you performed an FTP download, check the site to determine if it was necessary to perform a BIN (binary) transfer — and if so, make sure that you did so (To perform a binary transfer, enter "BIN" at the "ftp>" prompt). You should also verify any checksums provided for downloaded files.

To ensure that the OpenSSH content is complete and has not been corrupted in transit or maliciously modified, the PGP signature should also be checked. Note that a trojaned version of OpenSSH has previously been placed on hacked mirror FTP sites (See CERT CA-2002-24 for details). Unfortunately, the whereabouts of the OpenSSH public key are not well publicized at the time of this writing. The public key currently used to sign OpenSSH belongs to Damien Miller (Personal Key) <djm@mindrot.org> and may be retrieved from PGP key servers using id **86FF9C48**. The following example commands use the open source GNU Privacy Guard (GPG) from http://www.gnupg.org/.

The key is also available from the mirror FTP sites, however, if you retrieve it from the same FTP server from which you downloaded the software, you run the risk that both have been maliciously altered. Once the key is imported, the tar bundle can be verified. It is not necessary to assign any trust to the key.

```
$> gpg --keyserver wwwkeys.pgp.net --recv-keys 86FF9C48

$> gpg --list-keys 86FF9C48
pub   1024D/86FF9C48 2001-02-26 Damien Miller (Personal Key) <djm@mindrot.org>
sub   2048g/AA2B1C41 2001-02-26
```

```
$> gpg --verify openssh-3.5p1.tar.gz.sig openssh-3.5p1.tar.gz
gpg: Signature made Thu Oct  3 21:34:43 2002 EDT using DSA key ID 86FF9C48
gpg: Good signature from "Damien Miller (Personal Key) <djm@mindrot.org>"

Could not find a valid trust path to the key.  Let's see whether we can assign some missing owner
trust values.

No path leading to one of our keys found.

gpg: WARNING:     This key is not certified with a trusted signature!
gpg:              There is no indication that the signature belongs to the owner.
gpg: Fingerprint: 3981 992A 1523 ABA0 79DB  FC66 CE8E CB03 86FF 9C48
```

Many open-source tools provide a significant amount of verbose output when they are installed, so it can be easy to overlook error messages. Therefore, it's a good idea to review any install messages/logs for the pre-requisite software if you still have them. If these are not available, then you may still be able to validate the installations -- most of the open-source tools come with helpful installation/configuration documentation. Check for INSTALL and README files within the directories where you stored the source code for each package. These files frequently provide good detail and can be of great help. For example, notice the INSTALL and README files that are provided with the OpenSSL distribution:

```
# pwd
/usr/local/openssl-0.9.6g
# ls
CHANGES          MacOS           apps      include        perl
CHANGES.SSLeay   Makefile        bugs      install.com    rehash.time
Configure        Makefile.org    certs     libRSAglue.a   rsaref
FAQ              Makefile.ssl    config    libcrypto.a    shlib
INSTALL          NEWS            crypto    libssl.a       ssl
INSTALL.MacOS    PROBLEMS        demos     makevms.com    test
INSTALL.VMS      README          doc       ms             times
INSTALL.W32      README.ENGINE   e_os.h    openssl.doxy   tools
LICENSE          VMS             e_os2.h   openssl.spec   util
```

Action 5.1.2 - Verify OpenSSH commands are in the UNIX search path

If you get a "not found" error when trying to invoke one of the OpenSSH executables (ssh, slogin, scp, sftp, etc), then make sure that the UNIX PATH environment variable includes the location of the executables; otherwise the OpenSSH commands' location will have to be provided when the executables are invoked. For example:

```
$ ssh server.example.com
ssh: not found
$ echo $PATH
/usr/sbin:/usr/bin:/usr/dt/bin:/usr/openwin/bin:/bin:/usr/ucb:/usr/ccs/bin
```

To update the search PATH, first verify the location of the executables. For example, if you installed the executables in the /usr/local/bin directory, the following commands in a Bourne-, Korn-, or Z-Shell will ensure that this directory will be searched:

```
$ PATH=$PATH:/usr/local/bin; export PATH
$ echo $PATH
/usr/sbin:/usr/bin:/usr/dt/bin:/usr/openwin/bin:/bin:/usr/ucb:/usr/ccs/bin:/usr/local/bin
```

A subsequent SSH attempt is now successful:

```
$ ssh server.example.com
sshuser@server.example.com's password: *******
Last login: Mon Feb 17 14:05:03 2003 from client.example.com
$
```

Action 5.1.3 - Utilize verbose option to OpenSSH commands

Sometimes the -v verbose option available with most of the OpenSSH commands can provide insight. This option provides much more detail than is normally received. For example, here is the previous connection attempt using the -v flag:

```
$ ssh -v server.example.com
OpenSSH_3.5p1, SSH protocols 1.5/2.0, OpenSSL 0x0090607f
debug1: Reading configuration data /usr/local/etc/ssh_config
debug1: Rhosts Authentication disabled, originating port will not be trusted.
debug1: ssh_connect: needpriv 0
debug1: Connecting to server.example.com [172.16.121.6] port 22.
debug1: Connection established.
debug1: identity file /home/sshuser/.ssh/id_rsa type 1
debug1: Remote protocol version 2.0, remote software version OpenSSH_3.4p1
debug1: match: OpenSSH_3.4p1 pat OpenSSH*
debug1: Enabling compatibility mode for protocol 2.0
debug1: Local version string SSH-2.0-OpenSSH_3.5p1
debug1: SSH2_MSG_KEXINIT sent
debug1: SSH2_MSG_KEXINIT received
debug1: kex: server->client aes128-cbc hmac-md5 none
```

```
debug1: kex: client->server aes128-cbc hmac-md5 none
debug1: SSH2_MSG_KEX_DH_GEX_REQUEST sent
debug1: expecting SSH2_MSG_KEX_DH_GEX_GROUP
debug1: dh_gen_key: priv key bits set: 113/256
debug1: bits set: 1602/3191
debug1: SSH2_MSG_KEX_DH_GEX_INIT sent
debug1: expecting SSH2_MSG_KEX_DH_GEX_REPLY
debug1: Host 'server.example.com' is known and matches the RSA host key.
debug1: Found key in /home/sshuser/.ssh/known_hosts:1
debug1: bits set: 1595/3191
debug1: ssh_rsa_verify: signature correct
debug1: kex_derive_keys
debug1: newkeys: mode
debug1: SSH2_MSG_NEWKEYS sent
debug1: waiting for SSH2_MSG_NEWKEYS
debug1: newkeys: mode 0
debug1: SSH2_MSG_NEWKEYS received
debug1: done: ssh_kex2.
debug1: send SSH2_MSG_SERVICE_REQUEST
debug1: service_accept: ssh-userauth
debug1: got SSH2_MSG_SERVICE_ACCEPT
debug1: authentications that can continue: publickey,password,keyboard-interactive
debug1: next auth method to try is publickey
debug1: try pubkey: /export/home/sshuser/.ssh/id_rsa
debug1: authentications that can continue: publickey,password,keyboard-interactive
debug1: next auth method to try is keyboard-interactive
debug1: authentications that can continue: publickey,password,keyboard-interactive
debug1: next auth method to try is password
sshuser@server.example.com's password
```

As you can see, the verbose flag provides helpful debugging information - in this example, the client "knows" about the server (i.e. this is not the first SSH connection attempt), the client and server have "negotiated" to use the SSHv2 protocol, and public key authentication has failed (possibly this type of authentication has not yet been configured or the permissions for the file containing the private key have not been set to a secure level), so the UNIX password authentication is tried next (default behavior for SSH authentication).

> **Tech Tip**
> You should note that multiple -v options are supported - e.g. `ssh -vv server.example.com`.
> For each additional `-v` provided, more verbose output will be provided.

Action 5.1.4 - Utilize OpenSSH server daemon log

By default, the OpenSSH server daemon (sshd) logs certain information, such as authentication failures, to the UNIX syslog facility. These messages can sometimes provide insight, especially if the problem is just an incorrect password or passphrase. For example, here is an entry indicating an authentication failure on an OpenSSH server:

```
Feb 19 13:37:50 server.example.com sshd[10024]: [ID 800047 auth.crit] fatal: Timeout before
    authentication for 172.16.121.16.
```

You can get much more verbose output in the OpenSSH server log file by restarting the sshd daemon with the -d (debug) command line option. For example, on the OpenSSH server:

```
# /usr/local/sbin/sshd -d &
[1]      14027
```

If you use the -d flag, be prepared to wade through a lot of detail. The following is the verbose output from a client connection whereby the public key authentication failed and therefore UNIX password authentication was used (which is the default sshd behavior):

```
debug1: sshd version OpenSSH_3.4p1
debug1: read PEM private key done: type RSA
debug1: private host key: #0 type 1 RSA
debug1: read PEM private key done: type DSA
debug1: private host key: #1 type 2 DSA
debug1: Bind to port 22 on ::.
Server listening on :: port 22.
debug1: Bind to port 22 on 0.0.0.0.
Server listening on 0.0.0.0 port 22.
debug1: Server will not fork when running in debugging mode.
Connection from 172.16.121.16 port 33672
debug1: Client protocol version 2.0; client software version OpenSSH_3.5p1
debug1: match: OpenSSH_3.5p1 pat OpenSSH*
Enabling compatibility mode for protocol 2.0
debug1: Local version string SSH-2.0-OpenSSH_3.4p1
debug1: list_hostkey_types: ssh-rsa,ssh-dss
debug1: SSH2_MSG_KEXINIT sent
debug1: SSH2_MSG_KEXINIT received
debug1: kex: client->server aes128-cbc hmac-md5 none
debug1: kex: server->client aes128-cbc hmac-md5 none
debug1: SSH2_MSG_KEX_DH_GEX_REQUEST received
debug1: SSH2_MSG_KEX_DH_GEX_GROUP sent
debug1: dh_gen_key: priv key bits set: 133/256
debug1: bits set: 1590/3191
debug1: expecting SSH2_MSG_KEX_DH_GEX_INIT
```

```
debug1: bits set: 1617/3191
debug1: SSH2_MSG_KEX_DH_GEX_REPLY sent
debug1: kex_derive_keys
debug1: newkeys: mode 1
debug1: SSH2_MSG_NEWKEYS sent
debug1: waiting for SSH2_MSG_NEWKEYS
debug1: newkeys: mode 0
debug1: SSH2_MSG_NEWKEYS received
debug1: KEX done
debug1: userauth-request for user sshuser service ssh-connection method none
debug1: attempt 0 failures 0
Failed none for sshuser from 172.16.121.16 port 33672 ssh2
Failed none for sshuser from 172.16.121.16 port 33672 ssh2
debug1: userauth-request for user sshuser service ssh-connection method publickey
debug1: attempt 1 failures 1
debug1: test whether pkalg/pkblob are acceptable
debug1: temporarily_use_uid: 1009/150 (e=0)
debug1: trying public key file /home/sshuser/.ssh/authorized_keys
debug1: matching key found: file /home/sshuser/.ssh/authorized_keys, line 1
Found matching RSA key: a4:93:99:99:29:9f:41:9d:af:21:54:b6:8f:3e:ce:c6
debug1: restore_uid
Postponed publickey for sshuser from 172.16.121.16 port 33672 ssh2
debug1: userauth-request for user sshuser service ssh-connection method keyboard-interactive
debug1: attempt 2 failures 1
debug1: keyboard-interactive devs
debug1: auth2_challenge: user=sshuser devs=
debug1: kbdint_alloc: devices ''
Failed keyboard-interactive for sshuser from 172.16.121.16 port 33672 ssh2
debug1: userauth-request for user sshuser service ssh-connection method password
debug1: attempt 3 failures 2
Failed password for sshuser from 172.16.121.16 port 33672 ssh2Failed password for sshuser from 172.16.121.16 port 33672 ssh2
debug1: userauth-request for user sshuser service ssh-connection method password
debug1: attempt 4 failures 3
Accepted password for sshuser from 172.16.121.16 port 33672 ssh2
debug1: monitor_child_preauth: sshuser has been authenticated by privileged process
Accepted password for sshuser from 172.16.121.16 port 33672 ssh2
```

```
debug1: newkeys: mode 0
debug1: newkeys: mode 1
debug1: Entering interactive session for SSH2.
debug1: fd 4 setting O_NONBLOCK
debug1: fd 5 setting O_NONBLOCK
debug1: server_init_dispatch_20
debug1: server_input_channel_open: ctype session rchan 0 win 65536 max 16384
debug1: input_session_request
debug1: channel 0: new [server-session]
debug1: session_new: init
debug1: session_new: session 0
debug1: session_open: channel 0
debug1: session_open: session 0: link with channel 0
debug1: server_input_channel_open: confirm session
debug1: server_input_channel_req: channel 0 request pty-req reply 0
debug1: session_by_channel: session 0 channel 0
debug1: session_input_channel_req: session 0 req pty-req
debug1: Allocating pty.
debug1: session_new: init
debug1: session_new: session 0
debug1: session_pty_req: session 0 alloc /dev/pts/22
debug1: server_input_channel_req: channel 0 request x11-req reply 0
debug1: session_by_channel: session 0 channel 0
debug1: session_input_channel_req: session 0 req x11-req
debug1: fd 12 setting O_NONBLOCK
debug1: channel 1: new [X11 inet listener]
debug1: fd 13 setting O_NONBLOCK
debug1: channel 2: new [X11 inet listener]
debug1: server_input_channel_req: channel 0 request shell reply 0
debug1: session_by_channel: session 0 channel 0
debug1: session_input_channel_req: session 0 req shell
```

> **Tech Tip**
> Multiple -d options can be utilized when launching the OpenSSH daemon - e.g. `/usr/local/sbin/sshd -d -d &` to provide an additional level of debugging detail.

Action 5.1.5 – Run the OpenSSH Server in foreground verbose mode

Running the server in foreground debug mode (`-D -d`) is very useful for debugging a wide variety of connection problems. When run in the foreground, the server will need to be restarted for each connection attempt:

```
# /usr/local/sbin/sshd -D -d

debug1: Seeding random number generator
debug1: sshd version OpenSSH_3.0.1p1
debug1: private host key: #0 type 0 RSA1
debug1: read PEM private key done: type RSA
debug1: private host key: #1 type 1 RSA
debug1: read PEM private key done: type DSA
debug1: private host key: #2 type 2 DSA
debug1: Bind to port 22 on 192.168.102.12.
Server listening on 192.168.102.12 port 22.
debug1: Bind to port 22 on 216.55.177.197.
Server listening on 192.168.102.12 port 22.
debug1: Server will not fork when running in debugging mode.
Connection from 10.10.102.84 port 1446
debug1: Client protocol version 2.0; client software version PuTTY-Release-0.53b
debug1: no match: PuTTY-Release-0.53b
Enabling compatibility mode for protocol 2.0
debug1: Local version string SSH-2.0-OpenSSH_3.0.1p1
debug1: Rhosts Authentication disabled, originating port 1446 not trusted.
debug1: list_hostkey_types: ssh-rsa,ssh-dss
debug1: SSH2_MSG_KEXINIT sent
debug1: SSH2_MSG_KEXINIT received
debug1: kex: client->server 3des-cbc hmac-sha1 none
debug1: kex: server->client 3des-cbc hmac-sha1 none
debug1: SSH2_MSG_KEX_DH_GEX_REQUEST_OLD received
debug1: SSH2_MSG_KEX_DH_GEX_GROUP sent
debug1: dh_gen_key: priv key bits set: 193/384
debug1: bits set: 1595/3191
debug1: expecting SSH2_MSG_KEX_DH_GEX_INIT
debug1: bits set: 1599/3191
debug1: SSH2_MSG_KEX_DH_GEX_REPLY sent
debug1: kex_derive_keys
debug1: newkeys: mode 1
debug1: SSH2_MSG_NEWKEYS sent
debug1: waiting for SSH2_MSG_NEWKEYS
debug1: newkeys: mode 0
debug1: SSH2_MSG_NEWKEYS received
debug1: KEX done
```

Step 5.2 - Troubleshooting Common OpenSSH Errors/Problems

Action 5.2.1 - Receiving "Connection refused" error when attempting to connect

```
$ ssh server.example.com
ssh: connect to host server.example.com port 22: Connection refused
```

1. Make sure that the sshd daemon is running on the OpenSSH server and that it is functional on the network. For example, to verify from an SSH client that the sshd daemon is functional:

```
$ telnet server.example.com 22
Trying 172.16.121.6...
Connected to server.example.com
Escape character is '^]'.
SSH-2.0-OpenSSH_3.4p1
```

If you do not see the OpenSSH version string and/or receive "Connection refused", proceed with the following checks.

2. Make sure that the OpenSSH Server is listening on the standard port 22. If possible, check the `/usr/local/etc/sshd_config` on the OpenSSH server to determine if a different port is being used to run the sshd daemon. If the default port 22 has been changed on the OpenSSH server, you will also need to modify the default port in the client's `/usr/local/etc/ssh_config` file. If you don't want to change the `ssh_config` file permanently, another option is to specify the OpenSSH server's port number as a flag to the client's ssh command. For example:

```
$ ssh server.example.com -p 1212
```

3. Check to see if the OpenSSH server is also running TCP Wrappers – and perhaps you have been denied access? If this is the case, there should be messages in the OpenSSH server's syslog indicating so. Also, check for the presence and contents of `/etc/host.deny` and `/etc/host.allow` files.

Action 5.2.2 - Receiving "permission denied" error when attempting to connect using standard UNIX authentication

```
$ ssh server.example.com
sshuser@server.example.com's password: ********
Permission denied, please try again.
sshuser@server.example.com's password: ********
```

1. Did you mistype the account or password name? Is the "Caps Lock" key toggled on?

2. Verify that the account to which you are attempting to connect on the OpenSSH server is active on the server and that the password has not expired or the account deactivated for whatever reason.

3. Did anyone else use this account and/or know the password? If so, verify that it has not been changed.

Action 5.2.3 - Receiving password prompt when expecting public key passphrase prompt

Receiving:
```
$ ssh server.example.com
sshuser@server.example.com's password:
```

Expecting:
```
$ ssh server.example.com
Enter passphrase for key '/home/sshuser/.ssh/id_rsa':
```

(Keep in mind, OpenSSH by default tries public key authentication before it tries host-based (i.e. UNIX password) authentication -- so, as long as you know the UNIX password, you should still be able to connect in a secure manner, assuming that password authentication is still enabled. See the man page for the ssh command)

1. Make sure that the `authorized_keys` file is in the proper location, `$HOME/.ssh/authorized_keys`, on the OpenSSH server (if the `$HOME/.ssh/authorized_keys` file exists, the OpenSSH server will, by default, try public key authentication first - see man page for sshd).

2. Make sure that the corresponding private key exists on the client from which you are connecting.

3. Make sure the owner of the `$HOME/.ssh/authorized_keys` file is the account to which you are attempting to connect.

4. Make sure that the permissions of the `$HOME/.ssh` directory and the authorized_keys file do NOT allow "write" privileges by "group" or "other". For example:
```
$ pwd
/home/sshuser
$ cd .ssh
$ chmod 744 .
$ chmod 644 ./authorized_keys
$ ls -l
total 6
-rw-r--r--   1 sshuser    admin    223 Apr 14 16:44 authorized_keys
-rw-r--r--   1 sshuser    admin    230 Apr  6 01:17 known_hosts
-rw-------   1 sshuser    admin   1024 Apr  6 01:28 prng_seed
$ ls -ld
drwxr--r--   2 sshuser    admin    512 Apr  6 01:17 .
```

5. Check the OpenSSH server's `sshd_config` file, located by default in `/usr/local/etc/sshd_config`. There are 3 entries in this file that can affect the availability/functionality of public key authentication:
```
RSAAuthentication yes          (applicable to SSHv1)
PubkeyAuthentication yes       (applicable to SSHv2)
AuthorizedKeysFile    .ssh/authorized_keys
```
By default each of these entries is commented out and ignored, as indicated by the "#" preceding each entry. The OpenSSH default is to allow public key authentication (and to use it first), so if this file has not been modified since the install, then your problem is not here. However, if either of the first two entries has been set to "no" or the default location of the `authorized_keys` file has been changed, this may be the source of the problem.

It should be noted that the "RSAAuthentication" setting applies for SSHv1, while "PubkeyAuthentication" applies for SSHv2 — both can be allowed independently.

Action 5.2.4 - Getting immediate disconnect when attempting connection
```
$ ssh server.example.com
Connection closed by 192.168.121.6
```

1. Check the OpenSSH servers' `$HOME/.ssh/authorized_keys` file and **make sure that there are no carriage-returns imbedded within the individual public key string** - each public key entry must be one-continuous line. The only carriage-returns should be between public key entries.

Action 5.2.5 - Passphrase is no longer valid and you know you didn't change it

```
$ ssh server.example.com
Enter passphrase for key '/home/sshuser/.ssh/id_rsa':
Enter passphrase for key '/home/sshuser/.ssh/id_rsa':
sshuser@server.example.com's password:
```

1. Do others share this account with you? (Hopefully not!)

2. Check the `$HOME/.ssh/authorized_keys` file to make sure it has not been tampered with or accidentally modified. If the file has been modified, you will need to remove or correct any wrong entries or in worst case, you may need to use "ssh-keygen" to generate a new public/private key pair.

Action 5.2.6 – Unexpected Host Key not cached

The first time your SSH client connects with an OpenSSH server you will be prompted to verify the authenticity of the server host key. If this is the first time the client system has connected to the specific server as the current user, then the message should be expected. If the message appears at a subsequent connection time, this may indicate some form of malicious activity.

It is recommended that the host key be verified via an alternate trusted communication channel, such as contacting a local administrator by phone, connecting to the same server from a different and already verified communication channel, or checking the cache of other client systems which have verified the host key. UNIX SSH clients typically store the cache in `$HOME/.ssh/known_hosts` (although this can be changed in the OpenSSH configuration) while PuTTY stores the cache in the Windows registry under the current user hive.

The SSH protocol cannot fully protect you if you fail to verify that you are connecting to the correct server with the authentic host key. It is important that administrators explain that connecting to server.example.com doesn't necessarily result in a connection to the expected server, if an attacker has succeeded in corrupting the IP routing or the DNS cache. Action 5.2.7 provides additional information and references.

Sample UNIX OpenSSH client:

```
$ ssh server.example.com
The authenticity of host 'server.example.com (192.168.1.10)' can't be established.
RSA key fingerprint is dd:7b:0d:55:f3:ca:b7:ad:2c:7f:d1:a5:ab:17:b5:67.
Are you sure you want to continue connecting (yes/no)?
```

If this is not the first time you have connected to the server, you should consider the following questions, then re-verify the authenticity of the server host key, as if it were a first time connection.

1. Is it possible previous connections were from a different client?

2. Is it possible previous connections were from a different user login on the client?

3. Is it possible the SSH key cache has been cleared for legitimate administrative reasons such as the user account being recreated, or the home directory or user registry has been cleaned out?

4. Has the name or IP address of the server changed?

5. Is the SSH client connecting with a different protocol (SSHv1 vs. SSHv2) than previously? This could be happening incidentally, as specified by the user, or forced as part of an attack. To verify, check the PuTTY event logs or re-run the UNIX SSH client with the -v (verbose) option.

> **Important Recommendation:**
> *It is strongly encouraged that you disable the usage of the SSHv1 protocol on all clients and server configurations and force usage of the SSHv2 protocol. The SSHv1 protocol has known deficiencies that increase the risk of insertion and man-in-the-middle attacks.*

Action 5.2.7 – Cached Host Key does not match

If you connect to an OpenSSH server and get a message indicating that the cached host key does not match, there are several things to consider carefully. Here is an example of one such occurrence:

```
$ ssh server.example.com
@@@@@@@@@@@@@@@@@@@@@@@@@@@@@@@@@@@@@@@@@@@@@@@@@@@@@@@@@
@    WARNING: REMOTE HOST IDENTIFICATION HAS CHANGED!    @
@@@@@@@@@@@@@@@@@@@@@@@@@@@@@@@@@@@@@@@@@@@@@@@@@@@@@@@@@
IT IS POSSIBLE THAT SOMEONE IS DOING SOMETHING NASTY!
Someone could be eavesdropping on you right now (man-in-the-middle attack)!
It is also possible that the RSA host key has just been changed.
The fingerprint for the RSA key sent by the remote host is
dd:7b:0d:55:f3:ca:b7:ad:2c:7f:d1:a5:ab:17:b5:67.
Please contact your system administrator.
Add correct host key in /home/sshuser/.ssh/known_hosts to get rid of this message.
Offending key in /home/sshuser/.ssh/known_hosts:5
RSA host key for server.example.com has changed and you have requested strict checking.
Host key verification failed.
```

It is possible that you are experiencing what is known as a man-in-the-middle (MITM) attack; however there are other possibilities. In any case, it is important that SSH users be aware of the possibilities and know how to respond to this message. It is also important that the answer be verified rather than assumed. Here are some other possibilities to consider when this message occurs:

1. Someone has upgraded the OpenSSH server and regenerated the host keys in the process.

2. A different server is answering to the name and/or IP address due to intentional administrative changes or server load balancing.

3. The SSH connection has been redirected to another server, possibly with malicious intent. The MITM attack can be accomplished by attacks at different protocol levels, including DNS, IP routing and ARP.

See Julian Beling's GSEC practical for an excellent introduction to SSH MITM attacks. http://www.giac.org/practical/Julian_Beling_GSEC.doc
Richard Silverman's reply to Dug Song's dsniff release is also good reading. http://sysadmin.oreilly.com/news/silverman_1200.html

Section 6 - Advanced SSH Topics

Problem: Since many programs use services that send clear-text data over the network, it is desirable to find something that can be used to encrypt the network traffic for these services while minimizing any change to end users. SSH provides this functionality with port forwarding.

Step 6.1 Port Forwarding

Port forwarding allows a user to create an encrypted session from a client to a remote server for any TCP-based service by tunneling the service through SSH. Of course, this requires that the user have an account on the remote server and that the OpenSSH daemon is running on the server.

OpenSSH allows you to configure port forwarding from the command line using the `-L` option as shown below:

```
$ ssh -L local_port:remote_host:remote_port hostname
```

where

`local_port` = the port on the local host that will listen for local connections
`remote_host` = the remote host where the service you wish to port forward is located
`remote_port` = the port on which the remote host is listening for the service you wish to port forward
`hostname` = the host to which you are creating an SSH session to

The local port can be any port on the local machine that does not already have a listening service. If you wish to utilize a reserved port (below 1024), you must have root privileges on your local machine.

As long as the service you wish to forward through the SSH tunnel uses TCP to communicate, such as HTTP, FTP, POP3 or SMTP, you should be able to use port forwarding to encrypt the service. The following example will demonstrate how to use SSH port forwarding to check your email on a remote UNIX server from a local UNIX machine. This example will use SMTP for sending email and POP3 for retrieving email. These services listen on TCP ports 25 and 110, respectively.

> **NOTE:** *The machine which becomes the terminating point for your port forwarding tunnel does not have to be the machine to which you create an SSH tunnel. For example, you could SSH to* `server1.example.com` *and create an SSH port forwarding tunnel to* `server2.example.com` *with the following command:*
>
> ```
> $ ssh -L 25:server2.example.com:25 server1.example.com
> ```
>
> *This will work as long as* `server1.example.com` *can contact* `server2.example.com`.
>
> *Make sure you realize that if you do this, your traffic will only be SSH-encrypted from your local machine to* `server1.example.com` - *it will be in clear-text from* `server1.example.com` *to* `server2.example.com`.

Action 6.1.1 – Use OpenSSH to set up port forwarding
We first need to connect to the remote machine `server.example.com` and set up port forwarding by running the following command:

```
$ ssh -L 1125:server.example.com:25 -L 1230:server.example.com:110 -l sshuser server.example.com
```

This command tells OpenSSH to open an SSH session to remote host `server.example.com` as user sshuser and to set up port forwarding so anything connecting on local port 1125 will be forwarded to remote port 25 and anything connecting on local port 1230 will be forwarded to remote port 110. The local ports could have been any that do not already have a listening service.

If we had wanted to use any of the reserved ports below 1024, we would have had to be root in order to set up the SSH port forwarding. If your mail client cannot be set up to talk on non-standard ports, you may be required to set up port forwarding as root.

If OpenSSH succeeds in making a connection to the remote host, you will be prompted for authentication to the remote host. After successfully authenticating to the remote host, you will be presented with a shell prompt. Port forwarding will be active until this session is closed.

Action 6.1.2 – Verify port forwarding is working
We know we have a shell session opened to the remote host, but how can we verify that port forwarding is active? This can be done using the `netstat` command. Using the `-an` options with `netstat` displays information about all services, including listening services, on the local machine. With this information, we can verify that port forwarding is configured properly.

- Open another shell prompt on the local machine.
- At the prompt, run the `netstat` command as follows:

```
$ netstat -an | more
```

(Piping the command through `more` will prevent the information from scrolling off the screen.) The following information should be displayed:

```
Active Internet connections (servers and established)
Proto Recv-Q Send-Q Local Address      Foreign Address     State

tcp        0      0 127.0.0.1:1125     0.0.0.0:*           LISTEN
tcp        0      0 127.0.0.1:1230     0.0.0.0:*           LISTEN

tcp        0      0 0.0.0.0:22         0.0.0.0:*           LISTEN
tcp        0      0 192.168.1.1:22     192.169.3.1:1189    ESTABLISHED
```

The amount of information displayed will vary depending on your operating system, but you should see ports 1125 and 1230 on the local host listening, as shown above.

Action 6.1.3 - Set up Pine to send and retrieve email through an SSH tunnel

One of the most common UNIX mail client programs is Pine. Pine is a command line program maintained by the University of Washington and can be downloaded from http://www.washington.edu/pine. The following are the steps required to configure Pine to exchange mail via an SSH tunnel:

- Launch Pine by entering the following at a command prompt on the local host:

    `$ pine`

- At the Pine main menu, press the **S** key to enter the setup screen.

- At the setup screen, press the **C** key to enter the configuration screen.

- The configuration screen is where we will configure email exchange. Press the **down key** until you reach the line entitled smtp-server and press **Enter**. At the prompt enter the following:

    `localhost:1125`

    and press **Enter**. This will tell Pine to use port 1125 on the local host to send email.

- Next, press the **down key** until you reach the line entitled inbox-path and press **Enter**. At the prompt, enter the following:

    `{localhost:1230/pop3/user=pop3_user}inbox`

    and press **Enter**. `Pop3_user` is the name of the POP3 user account from which you will be retrieving email. This will tell Pine to use the local host to check for POP3 email. ***Note: There is no space between the close curly bracket and `inbox`.***

- Once all of the information above is entered correctly, press the **E** key to exit the setup screen.

- Press **Y** when asked to commit changes.

Action 6.1.4 - Use Pine to retrieve email using port forwarding

- From the main menu of Pine, press the **L** key display the list of folders.

- In the list of folders, you will see the folder `INBOX`. Highlight `INBOX` and press **Enter**.

- If you are able to successfully connect and retrieve your email, you will be prompted for the password for the POP3 user for which you are attempting to retrieve email. Enter the password and press **Enter**. If you have any email, it should download now.

Action 6.1.5 - Use Pine to send email using port forwarding

- Press the **M** key to get back to the Pine main menu.

- Once you are back at the main menu, press the **C** key to compose a message.

- Enter all the relevant information to send the email, such as the recipient's address and the text of the message. Press Control-X to send the email. When prompted if you wish to send the email, press **Y**. If you do not receive any errors, the message has been sent through the port forwarding tunnel.

Problem: Many Windows e-mail programs send account ID, password and e-mail content over the network in clear-text.

Step 6.2 Using Port Forwarding Within PuTTY to Read Your E-mail Securely

Today there are a number of solutions available to provide protection against someone sniffing your credentials and data from the network, including VPN, SSL and SSH.

In this section, we will show how to utilize SSH port forwarding to securely send and retrieve email using IMAP and SMTP. Port forwarding allows you to run TCP based services in an SSH session from your local machine to a remote machine. By running the TCP based services in the SSH tunnel, all data going from your local machine to the remote machine endpoint is encrypted.

> NOTE: Keep in mind that by utilizing OpenSSH port forwarding, you are only encrypting the data as it goes from your local machine to your email server. The email is unencrypted as it travels from your email server to its destination server. To encrypt the contents of your email in this way, a program such as PGP or GPG is required.

Action 6.2.1 - Configure the initial PuTTY settings required for port forwarding
We first need to set up the initial connection settings to the remote mail server within PuTTY.
- First, double-click on the icon that was created for PuTTY or select it from the **Start Menu**.
- In the **Session** category, enter the hostname or IP address of the remote mail server to which you wish to connect in the **Host Name** field.
- Make sure **SSH** is selected under the **Protocol** field by clicking on the SSH radio button.

Action 6.2.2 - Configure IMAP port forwarding
- Select the **Connection->SSH->Tunnels** category on the left side window of the PuTTY configuration screen
- In the Port forwarding section of the right hand window, make sure the Local radio button is selected. To do this, click on **Local** at the bottom of the PuTTY Configuration screen, below the field marked Destination.
- Next, in the field marked `Source port`, enter 143, the default port for IMAP. Enter the hostname of the server on which your e-mail server is located in the field marked `Destination`, followed by a colon and 143, as shown below.

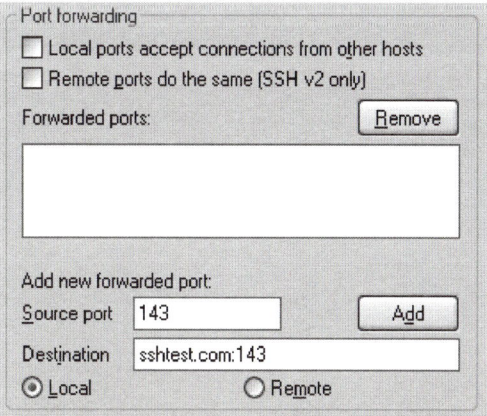

> **NOTE** – *The server and port of the machine you enter here does not have to be the machine to which you will be creating the SSH connection. If you enter a machine different from the one to which will connect via SSH, your data will be secured between the client and the SSH server, but not between the SSH server and the final destination. Only ports forwarded to the SSH server itself are encrypted.*

- Now click the **Add** button. As shown below, the box under the window marked **Forwarded ports** will show the address and port you entered earlier.

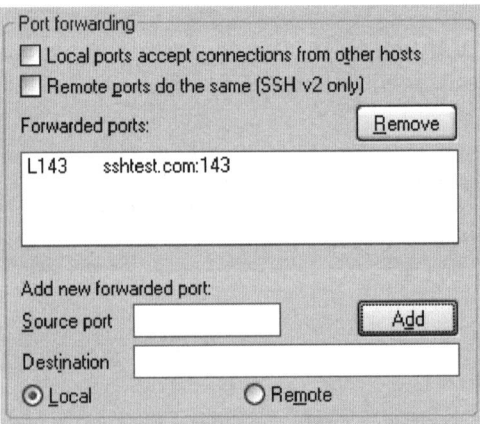

Action 6.2.3 - Configure SMTP port forwarding

Now we need to add the address of the computer to which we send our outgoing mail, utilizing SMTP. The default port for SMTP is 25.

- Enter 25 in the **Source port** field of the port forwarding section, as you did for IMAP.
- Next, in the **Destination** field, type the hostname or IP address of the computer where your SMTP server is located, followed by a colon and 25, as shown below.

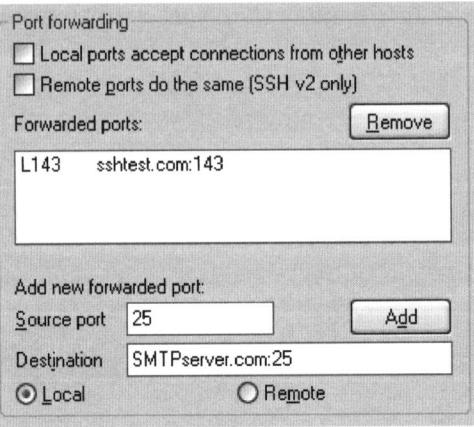

- Next, click the **Add** button - the address and port for the SMTP server will appear in the **Forwarded ports** box.

The **Port Forwarding** section of the PuTTY configuration should look like the screen below:

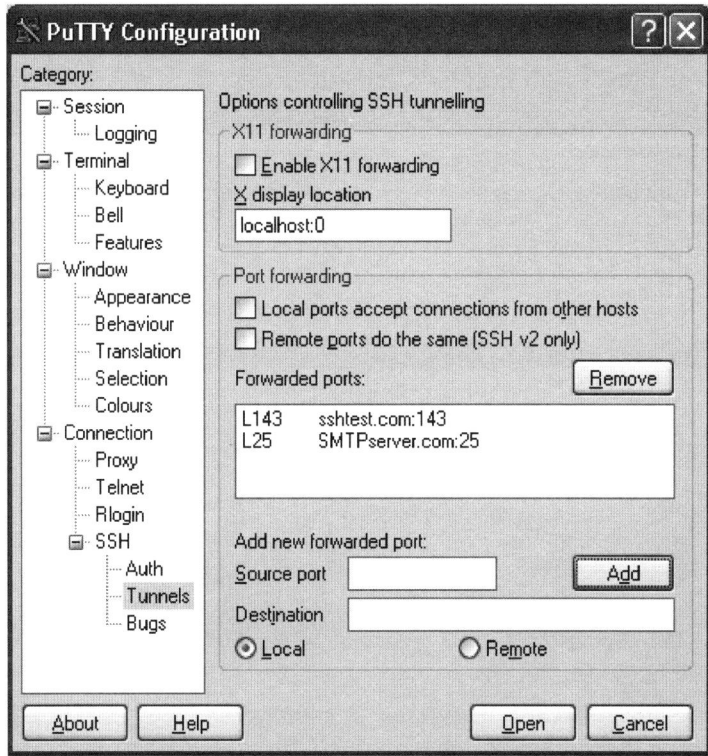

Action 6.2.4 - Create and verify the SSH connection and port forwarding

Now that PuTTY is configured to allow port forwarding, we need to connect to the remote server and verify that the local machine is listening on the correct ports.

- Click on the Open button at the bottom of the PuTTY configuration screen to open the connection to the remote machine.

- If the connection is successful, you will be prompted for authentication information. After you successfully enter your authentication credentials, you will be put at a shell prompt, just as if you had opened a normal SSH session to the remote machine.

(In fact, that is exactly what you have done - while the SSH port forwarding session is open, you are also connected interactively to the remote machine.)

Now that the connection is open, we need to verify that the local machine is listening on the ports we specified earlier:

- Click on the **Start Menu** and select **Run**. Enter `cmd` if you are running Windows NT/2000/XP or `command` if you are running Windows 9x/ME into the prompt given and click on the **OK** button. A Windows command prompt should appear.
- At the Windows command prompt, type in the command `netstat -an` and hit `enter`. Netstat is a program which will display statistics of the current TCP/IP connections on the local machine. The `-an` options tell `netstat` to display all connections and listening ports on your local machine. The output should be similar to that shown below.

(If the output scrolls by too quickly to read, pipe the command through `more` by running `netstat -an | more`. This will allow you to see the output one page at a time.)

```
Active Connections

  Proto  Local Address           Foreign Address         State
  TCP    0.0.0.0:135             0.0.0.0:0               LISTENING
  TCP    0.0.0.0:445             0.0.0.0:0               LISTENING
  TCP    0.0.0.0:1025            0.0.0.0:0               LISTENING
  TCP    0.0.0.0:1037            0.0.0.0:0               LISTENING
  TCP    0.0.0.0:1040            0.0.0.0:0               LISTENING
  TCP    0.0.0.0:1043            0.0.0.0:0               LISTENING
  TCP    0.0.0.0:1388            0.0.0.0:0               LISTENING
  TCP    0.0.0.0:9420            0.0.0.0:0               LISTENING
  TCP    192.168.1.10:1388       192.168.1.1:22          ESTABLISHED
  TCP    127.0.0.1:25            0.0.0.0:0               LISTENING
  TCP    127.0.0.1:143           0.0.0.0:0               LISTENING
  UDP    0.0.0.0:53              *:*
  UDP    0.0.0.0:135             *:*
  UDP    0.0.0.0:445             *:*
  UDP    0.0.0.0:1026            *:*
  UDP    0.0.0.0:1028            *:*
  UDP    0.0.0.0:1326            *:*
  UDP    0.0.0.0:44333           *:*
  UDP    127.0.0.1:123           *:*
```

As you can see, the output shows the open and listening connection for the local machine. You will want to look for lines similar to the ones highlighted above. The first highlighted line:

```
TCP      192.168.1.10:1388       192.168.1.1:22         ESTABLISHED
```

is the SSH connection from your local machine to the remote machine. You can tell this is an established connection by the **ESTABLISHED** state displayed in the fourth column.

The next two highlighted lines:

```
TCP      127.0.0.1:25            0.0.0.0:0              LISTENING
TCP      127.0.0.1:143           0.0.0.0:0              LISTENING
```

show us the port forwarding connections we have set up. The **LISTENING** state in the fourth column tells us that our local machine is listening on the ports specified in the second column. In this case, our local machine is listening on port 25, SMTP, and port 143, IMAP, at IP address 127.0.0.1. IP address 127.0.0.1 is the IP address of the loopback interface for our machine, also known as localhost.

Action 6.2.5 - Configure your email client
Now that we have port forwarding for SMTP and IMAP configured and the connection has been verified, we need to configure our email client to take advantage of port forwarding.

For this example, we will use Outlook 2000 as our email client. However, the process should apply to other email clients as well.

- Open Outlook, then click on the **Tools** menu and select **Accounts**.
- The window that appears is the list of all the accounts that are set up within Outlook. Click on the **Mail** tab.
- Select the mail account associated with the user account which is located on the server for which we have created the SSH connection and click on the **Properties** button.
- In the window that appears, select the **Servers** tab. This will display the servers that are configured for this email account.
- In the **Incoming Mail (IMAP)** field, enter `localhost`. This will tell Outlook to contact the local machine for which we have configured port forwarding to get email.
- In the **Outgoing Mail (SMTP)** field, enter `localhost`. This will tell Outlook to contact the local machine for which we have configured port forwarding to send email.

The properties for the mail account should now look like the screen shown below:

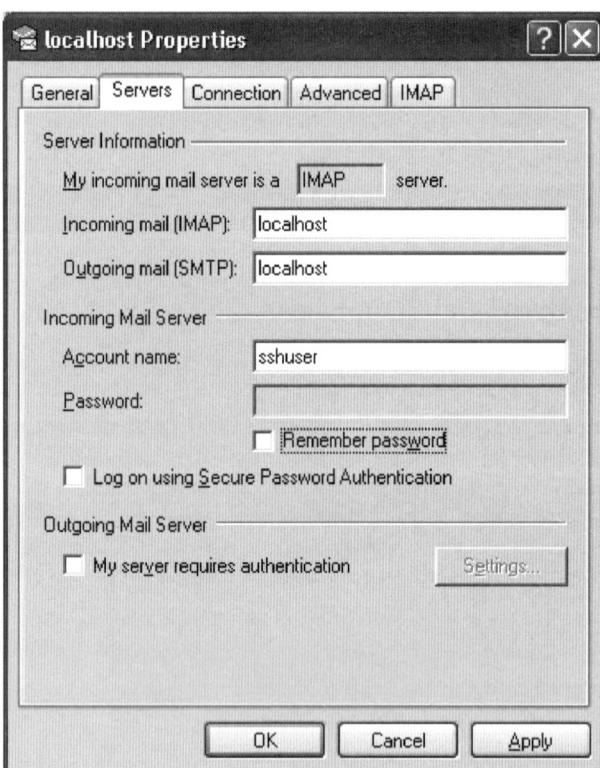

- Click the **OK** button to return to the list of accounts.
- Click the **Close** button to return to the main screen of Outlook.
- Send yourself an email to verify email is functional with the newly configured port forwarding and SSH tunnel.

Problem: Most every UNIX/Linux user will use X11, i.e. X-Windows, across a network for GUI-based applications. X11 is noted for its poor security and is a common target for attackers.

Step 6.3 X11 Forwarding

Action 6.3.1 - Utilize the OpenSSH X11 Forwarding Feature to Run X-Windows Applications Through a Secure Channel

OpenSSH provides X11 forwarding, which will automatically encrypt all X11 traffic, thereby reducing some of the security concerns with X. OpenSSH also improves the behind-the-scenes X-Windows authentication by encrypting the authentication process.

Another handy feature of X11 forwarding is that OpenSSH will automatically set the DISPLAY variable for you so that X applications are automatically displayed back to your local system.

There are a couple of SSH configuration options that are required in order for the remote OpenSSH server to enable X11 forwarding. Make sure these options are set in `sshd_config`:

```
X11Forwarding yes
X11UseLocalhost no
```

- To enable X11 forwarding for the SSH client, the `-X` parameter should be supplied at the command line to the SSH executable:

```
$ ssh -X -l sshuser server.example.com
sshuser@server.example.com's password: *********
Last login: Fri Dec 20 15:45:12 2002 from client.example.com
Sun Microsystems Inc.   SunOS 5.8       Generic February 2000
```

Once authentication has successfully taken place, the DISPLAY environment variable should be automatically set on the client, as shown below, to a display number that is higher than normal:

```
$ echo $DISPLAY
localhost:10.0
```

- Just as with normal X-Windows functionality, once you verify that the DISPLAY variable is set, you can launch an X application and the output of the application should appear on your local display:

```
$ xclock &
[1]     7324
$
```

Tech-Tip:
To help better understand the X11 forwarding feature of OpenSSH, it is helpful to keep in mind that X-Windows uses a "reverse" client/server design. In the example presented here, the X-Windows "server" is located on the SSH "client" whereas the X-Windows "client" is the SSH "server".

Once again, note that the SSH client never had to set the DISPLAY variable manually after it connected to the OpenSSH server. Without OpenSSH, we would have had to do this before running xclock, otherwise we would get "`Error: Can't open display`" or a similar error message.

Action 6.3.2 - Utilize the X11 forwarding feature in PuTTY to run X-Windows applications through a secure channel
Running X11 applications over a public or unsecured network can be dangerous since the X11 connection is not encrypted and therefore sensitive information could potentially be compromised. Additionally, running X11 applications through firewalls usually involves opening up multiple ports which firewall administrators typically do not like to open. To avoid these problems, X11 applications can be tunneled through SSH and onto a Windows computer:

> *NOTE: In order for the following to work, an X11 server, such as Cygwin's Xfree86 or Hummingbird's Exceed must be running on the Windows machine. The remote OpenSSH server must also be configured to allow X11 Forwarding – this can be accomplished by setting the X11Forwarding option in* `sshd_config` *to "Yes".*

- Double-click on the icon that was created for PuTTY or select it from the **Start Menu**.

- In the **Session** category, enter the hostname or IP address of the machine to which you will connect and run X11 applications.

- Make sure **SSH** is selected below the **Protocol** field by clicking on the **SSH** radio button.

- On the left hand window of the PuTTY configuration screen, select the **Connection->SSH->Tunnels** category.

- In the section labeled **X11 forwarding**, check the box marked **Enable X11 forwarding** and make sure the X **display location** box contains `localhost:0`, as shown below. The number after the colon in the **X display location** box, in this case 0, is known as the "X display number" and by default should be set to 0. However, if your local X11 server is not running on display number 0, set the appropriate display number in the **X display location** box.

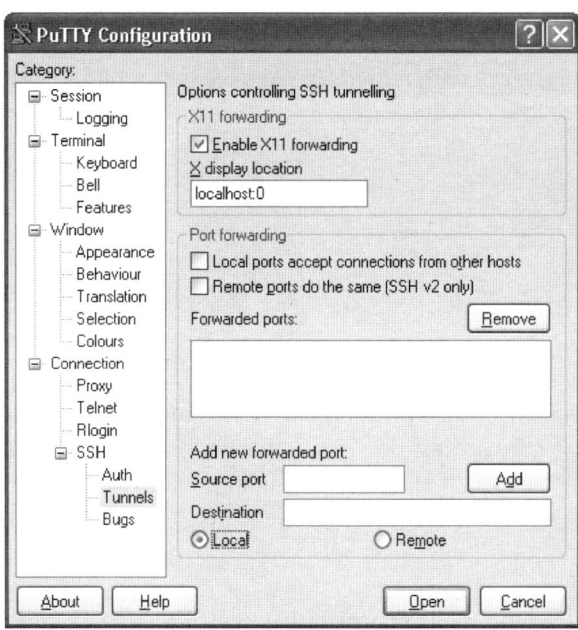

- Next, click on the **Open** button to open the connection to the remote machine. Enter your authentication information as prompted.

- After you have authenticated successfully to the remote machine you should see a shell prompt. The DISPLAY environment variable should now be set to the localhost using the display number previously specified by the X11DisplayOffset variable in the remote machine's `sshd_config` file. Verify your DISPLAY environment variable, as shown below:
  ```
  [sshuser@server.example.com]$ echo $DISPLAY
  localhost:10.0
  ```

- Run a small X11 application, such as `xclock`, to verify that X11 Forwarding is working correctly, as shown below.
  ```
  [sshuser@server.example.com]$ xclock &
  ```

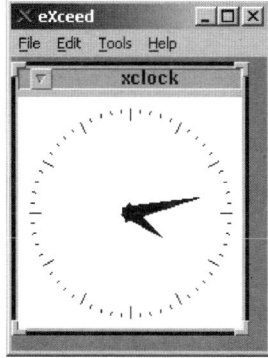

Conclusion

As with most great tools available to the security community, this publication has only scratched the surface with regards to OpenSSH's complete capabilities. The basics covered in this Step-by-Step guide are just that: basics. You now have the skills necessary to:

- Obtain, compile, install and configure OpenSSH
- Obtain, install and use a variety of Windows based SSH clients
- Initiate secure, interactive communication channels
- Transfer files securely using SSH
- Create, distribute, and securely utilize public/private key pairs

As a security practitioner, the responsibility is on you to be creative in your security solutions. The building blocks presented here will undoubtedly foster solutions, raise questions and initiate some heated discussions; all of which will contribute significantly to the profession *if you share* your solutions, questions or discussions. Defense in depth covers more than just the technical roadblocks we erect to thwart attackers. It also means building our professional communications so that the collective knowledge is shared, refined, and disseminated. So, you are encouraged to share your experience at the numerous available venues and to send email to openssh@sans.org.

The publishing team would like to thank you for your time in reading and using this publication. The time spent consolidating and distilling this information was done for one single reason: to help you secure your environment. OpenSSH is a powerful tool, one that should be used everywhere possible. It really is a necessary portion of our guiding principles:

1. If you don't need it, don't run it.
2. If you must run it, run it securely and keep it patched

Now that you have the knowledge, it's time to get busy. Use this book, implement OpenSSH, and be safe. Where are you going to disable telnet today?

Appendix — Sample sshd_config File

The following is a sample sshd_config file that contains descriptions for many of the options available for OpenSSH. Many of these descriptions were taken directly from the man page for sshd.

> **Note: Some of the settings specified below may be machine- or installation-specific, so please read through the descriptions for each option to make sure you understand each of the settings before you implement them.**

```
# Specifies whether an AFS token may be forwarded to the server.
# Default is "yes".
#AFSTokenPassing

# This keyword can be followed by a list of group name patterns,
# separated by spaces.  If specified, login is allowed only for
# users whose primary group or supplementary group list matches one
# of the patterns.  '*' and '?' can be used as wildcards in the
# patterns.  Only group names are valid; a numerical group ID is
# not recognized.  By default, login is allowed for all groups.
AllowGroups *

# Specifies whether TCP forwarding is permitted.  The default is
# "yes".  Note that disabling TCP forwarding does not improve
# security unless users are also denied shell access, as they can
# always install their own forwarders.
AllowTcpForwarding yes

# This keyword can be followed by a list of user name patterns,
# separated by spaces.  If specified, login is allowed only for
# users names that match one of the patterns.  '*' and '?' can be
# used as wildcards in the patterns.  Only user names are valid; a
# numerical user ID is not recognized.  By default, login is
# allowed for all users.  If the pattern takes the form USER@HOST
# then USER and HOST are separately checked, restricting logins to
# particular users from particular hosts.
AllowUsers *

# Specifies the file that contains the public keys that can be used
# for user authentication.  AuthorizedKeysFile may contain tokens
# of the form %T which are substituted during connection set-up.
```

```
# The following tokens are defined: %% is replaced by a literal
# '%', %h is replaced by the home directory of the user being
# authenticated and %u is replaced by the username of that user.
# After expansion, AuthorizedKeysFile is taken to be an absolute
# path or one relative to the user's home directory.  The default
# is ``.ssh/authorized_keys''.
AuthorizedKeysFile %h/.ssh/authorized_keys

# In some jurisdictions, sending a warning message before
# authentication may be relevant for getting legal protection.  The
# contents of the specified file are sent to the remote user before
# authentication is allowed.  This option is only available for
# protocol version 2.
Banner /etc/issue

# Specifies whether challenge response authentication is allowed.
# All authentication styles from login.conf(5) are supported.  The
# default is ``yes''.
ChallengeResponseAuthentication no

# Specifies the ciphers allowed for protocol version 2.  Multiple
# ciphers must be comma-separated.  The default is
#    ``aes128-cbc,3des-cbc,blowfish-cbc,cast128-cbc,arcfour,
#      aes192-cbc,aes256-cbc''
Ciphers aes128-cbc,3des-cbc,blowfish-cbc,cast128-cbc,arcfour,aes192-cbc,aes256-cbc

# Sets a timeout interval in seconds after which if no data has
# been received from the client, sshd will send a message through
# the encrypted channel to request a response from the client.  The
# default is 0, indicating that these messages will not be sent to
# the client.  This option applies to protocol version 2 only.
ClientAliveInterval 0

# Sets the number of client alive messages (see above) which may be
# sent without sshd receiving any messages back from the client. If
# this threshold is reached while client alive messages are being
# sent, sshd will disconnect the client, terminating the session.
# It is important to note that the use of client alive messages is
# very different from KeepAlive (below). The client alive messages
```

```
# are sent through the encrypted channel and therefore will not be
# spoofable. The TCP keepalive option enabled by KeepAlive is
# spoofable. The client alive mechanism is valuable when the client
# or server depend on knowing when a connection has become
# inactive.
# The default value is 3. If ClientAliveInterval (above) is set to
# 15, and ClientAliveCountMax is left at the default, unresponsive
# ssh clients will be disconnected after approximately 45 seconds.
ClientAliveCountMax 3

# This keyword can be followed by a list of group name patterns,
# separated by spaces.  Login is disallowed for users whose primary
# group or supplementary group list matches one of the patterns.
# `*' and `?' can be used as wildcards in the patterns.  Only group
# names are valid; a numerical group ID is not recognized.  By
# default, login is allowed for all groups.
#DenyGroups

# This keyword can be followed by a list of user name patterns,
# separated by spaces.  Login is disallowed for user names that
# match one of the patterns.  `*' and `?' can be used as wildcards
# in the patterns.  Only user names are valid; a numerical user ID
# is not recognized.  By default, login is allowed for all users.
# If the pattern takes the form USER@HOST then USER and HOST are
# separately checked, restricting logins to particular users from
# particular hosts.
#DenyUsers

# Specifies whether remote hosts are allowed to connect to ports
# forwarded for the client.  By default, sshd binds remote port
# forwardings to the loopback addresss.  This prevents other remote
# hosts from connecting to forwarded ports.  GatewayPorts can be
# used to specify that sshd should bind remote port forwardings to
# the wildcard address, thus allowing remote hosts to connect to
# forwarded ports.  The argument must be ``yes'' or ``no''.  The
# default is ``no''.
GatewayPorts no

# Specifies whether rhosts or /etc/hosts.equiv authentication
```

```
# together with successful public key client host authentication is
# allowed (hostbased authentication).  This option is similar to
# RhostsRSAAuthentication and applies to protocol version 2 only.
# The default is ``no''.
HostbasedAuthentication no

# Specifies a file containing a private host key used by SSH.  The
# default is /etc/ssh/sshuser_key for protocol version 1, and
# /etc/ssh/sshuser_rsa_key and /etc/ssh/sshuser_dsa_key for
# protocol version 2.  Note that sshd will refuse to use a file if
# it is group/world-accessible.  It is possible to have multiple
# host key files.  ``rsa1'' keys are used for version 1 and ``dsa''
# or ``rsa'' are used for version 2 of the SSH protocol.
HostKey /etc/ssh/sshuser_rsa_key
HostKey /etc/ssh/sshuser_dsa_key

# Specifies that .rhosts and .shosts files will not be used in
# RhostsAuthentication, RhostsRSAAuthentication or
# HostbasedAuthentication.
# /etc/hosts.equiv and /etc/ssh/shosts.equiv are still used.  The
# default is ``yes''.
IgnoreRhosts yes

# Specifies whether sshd should ignore the user's
# $HOME/.ssh/known_hosts during RhostsRSAAuthentication or
# HostbasedAuthentication.  The default is ``no''.
IgnoreUserKnownHosts no

# Specifies whether the system should send TCP keepalive messages
# to the other side.  If they are sent, death of the connection or
# crash of one of the machines will be properly noticed.  However,
# this means that connections will die if the route is down
# temporarily, and some people find it annoying.  On the other
# hand, if keepalives are not sent, sessions may hang indefinitely
# on the server, leaving ``ghost'' users and consuming server
# resources.
# The default is ``yes'' (to send keepalives), and the server will
# notice if the network goes down or the client host crashes.  This
# avoids infinitely hanging sessions.
```

```
# To disable keepalives, the value should be set to ``no''.
KeepAlive yes

# Specifies whether Kerberos authentication is allowed.  This can
# be in the form of a Kerberos ticket, or if PasswordAuthentication
# is yes, the password provided by the user will be validated
# through the Kerberos KDC.  To use this option, the server needs a
# Kerberos servtab which allows the verification of the KDC's
# identity.  Default is ``yes''.
#KerberosAuthentication

# If set then if password authentication through Kerberos fails
# then the password will be validated via any additional local
# mechanism such as /etc/passwd.  Default is ``yes''.
#KerberosOrLocalPasswd

# Specifies whether a Kerberos TGT may be forwarded to the server.
# Default is ``no'', as this only works when the Kerberos KDC is
# actually an AFS kaserver.
#KerberosTgtPassing

# Specifies whether to automatically destroy the user's ticket
# cache file on logout.  Default is ``yes''.
#KerberosTicketCleanup

# In protocol version 1, the ephemeral server key is automatically
# regenerated after this many seconds (if it has been used).  The
# purpose of regeneration is to prevent decrypting captured
# sessions by later breaking into the machine and stealing the
# keys.  The key is never stored anywhere.  If the value is 0, the
# key is never regenerated.  The default is 3600 (seconds).
#KeyRegenerationInterval

# Specifies whether PAM challenge response authentication is
# allowed. This allows the use of most PAM challenge response
# authentication modules, but it will allow password authentication
# regardless of whether PasswordAuthentication is disabled.  The
# default is ``no''.
PAMAuthenticationViaKbdInt no
```

```
# Specifies the port number that sshd listens on.  The default is
# 22.  Multiple options of this type are permitted.  See also
# ListenAddress.
Port 22

# Specifies the local addresses sshd should listen on.  The
# following forms may be used:
# ListenAddress host|IPv4_addr|IPv6_addr
# ListenAddress host|IPv4_addr:port
# ListenAddress [host|IPv6_addr]:port
# If port is not specified, sshd will listen on the address and all
# prior Port options specified. The default is to listen on all
# local addresses.  Multiple ListenAddress options are permitted.
# Additionally, any Port options must precede this option for non
# port qualified addresses.
ListenAddress 0.0.0.0

# The server disconnects after this time if the user has not
# successfully logged in.  If the value is 0, there is no time
# limit.  The default is 600 (seconds).
LoginGraceTime 60

# Gives the verbosity level that is used when logging messages from
# sshd.  The possible values are: QUIET, FATAL, ERROR, INFO,
# VERBOSE, DEBUG, DEBUG1, DEBUG2 and DEBUG3.  The default is INFO.
# DEBUG and DEBUG1 are equivalent.  DEBUG2 and DEBUG3 each specify
# higher levels of debugging output.  Logging with a DEBUG level
# violates the privacy of users and is not recommended.
LogLevel INFO

# Specifies the available MAC (message authentication code)
# algorithms.  The MAC algorithm is used in protocol version 2 for
# data integrity protection.  Multiple algorithms must be comma-
# separated.  The default is ``hmac-md5,hmac-sha1,hmac-
# ripemd160,hmac-sha1-96,hmac-md5-96''.
MACs hmac-md5,hmac-sha1,hmac-ripemd160,hmac-sha1-96,hmac-md5-96

# Specifies the maximum number of concurrent unauthenticated
```

```
# connections to the sshd daemon.  Additional connections will be
# dropped until authentication succeeds or the LoginGraceTime
# expires for a connection.  The default is 10.
# Alternatively, random early drop can be enabled by specifying the
# three colon separated values ``start:rate:full'' (e.g.,
# "10:30:60").  sshd will refuse connection attempts with a
# probability of ``rate/100'' (30%) if there are currently
# ``start'' (10) unauthenticated connections.  The probability
# increases linearly and all connection attempts are refused if the
# number of unauthenticated connections reaches ``full'' (60).
MaxStartups 10

# Specifies whether password authentication is allowed.  The
# default is ``yes''.
PasswordAuthentication yes

# When password authentication is allowed, it specifies whether the
# server allows login to accounts with empty password strings.  The
# default is ``no''.
PermitEmptyPasswords no

# Specifies whether root can login using ssh(1).  The argument must
# be ``yes'', ``without-password'', ``forced-commands-only'' or
# ``no''.  The default is ``yes''.
# If this option is set to ``without-password'' password
# authentication is disabled for root.
# If this option is set to ``forced-commands-only'' root login with
# public key authentication will be allowed, but only if the
# command option has been specified (which may be useful for taking
# remote backups even if root login is normally not allowed). All
# other authentication methods are disabled for root.
# If this option is set to ``no'' root is not allowed to login.
PermitRootLogin forced-commands-only

# Specifies the file that contains the process identifier of the
# sshd daemon.  The default is /var/run/sshd.pid.
PidFile /etc/ssh/sshd.pid

# Specifies whether sshd should print the date and time when the
```

```
# user last logged in.  The default is ``yes''.
PrintLastLog yes

# Specifies whether sshd should print /etc/motd when a user logs in
# interactively.  (On some systems it is also printed by the shell,
# /etc/profile, or equivalent.) The default is ``yes''.
PrintMotd yes

# Specifies the protocol versions sshd should support.  The
# possible values are ``1'' and ``2''.  Multiple versions must be
# comma-separated.  The default is ``2,1''.
Protocol 2

# Specifies whether public key authentication is allowed.  The
# default is ``yes''.  Note that this option applies to protocol
# version 2 only.
PubkeyAuthentication yes

# Specifies whether authentication using rhosts or /etc/hosts.equiv
# files is sufficient.  Normally, this method should not be
# permitted because it is insecure.  RhostsRSAAuthentication should
# be used instead, because it performs RSA-based host
# authentication in addition to normal rhosts or /etc/hosts.equiv
# authentication.  The default is ``no''.  This option applies to
# protocol version 1 only.
#RhostsAuthentication

# Specifies whether rhosts or /etc/hosts.equiv authentication
# together with successful RSA host authentication is allowed.  The
# default is ``no''.  This option applies to protocol version 1
# only.
#RhostsRSAAuthentication

# Specifies whether pure RSA authentication is allowed.  The
# default is ``yes''.  This option applies to protocol version 1
# only.
#RSAAuthentication

# Defines the number of bits in the ephemeral protocol version 1
```

```
# server key.  The minimum value is 512, and the default is 768.
#ServerKeyBits

# Specifies whether sshd should check file modes and ownership of
# the user's files and home directory before accepting login.  This
# is normally desirable because novices sometimes accidentally
# leave their directory or files world-writable.  The default is
# ``yes''.
StrictModes yes

# Configures an external subsystem (e.g., file transfer daemon).
# Arguments should be a subsystem name and a command to execute
# upon subsystem request.  The command sftp-server(8) implements
# the ``sftp'' file transfer subsystem.  By default no subsystems
# are defined.  Note that this option applies to protocol version 2
# only.
Subsystem sftp /opt/corp/local/openssh/sbin/sftp-server

# Gives the facility code that is used when logging messages from
# sshd.  The possible values are: DAEMON, USER, AUTH, LOCAL0,
# LOCAL1, LOCAL2, LOCAL3, LOCAL4, LOCAL5, LOCAL6, LOCAL7.  The
# default is AUTH.
SyslogFacility AUTH

# Specifies whether login(1) is used for interactive login
# sessions.  The default is ``no''.  Note that login(1) is never
# used for remote command execution.  Note also, that if this is
# enabled, X11Forwarding will be disabled because login(1) does not
# know how to handle xauth(1) cookies.
UseLogin no

# Specifies whether sshd should try to verify the remote host name
# and check that the resolved host name for the remote IP address
# maps back to the very same IP address.  The default is ``no''.
VerifyReverseMapping no

# Specifies the first display number available for sshd's X11
# forwarding.  This prevents sshd from interfering with real X11
```

```
# servers.  The default is 10.
X11DisplayOffset 10

# Specifies whether X11 forwarding is permitted.  The default is
# ``no''.  Note that disabling X11 forwarding does not improve
# security in any way, as users can always install their own
# forwarders.  X11 forwarding is automatically disabled if UseLogin
# is enabled.
X11Forwarding no

# Specifies whether sshd should bind the X11 forwarding server to
# the loopback address or to the wildcard address.  By default,
# sshd binds the forwarding server to the loopback address and sets
# the hostname part of the DISPLAY environment variable to
# ``localhost''.  This prevents remote hosts from connecting to the
# fake display.  However, some older X11 clients may not function
# with this configuration.  X11UseLocalhost may be set to ``no'' to
# specify that the forwarding server should be bound to the
# wildcard address.  The argument must be ``yes'' or ``no''.  The
# default is ``yes''.
X11UseLocalhost yes

# Specifies the location of the xauth(1) program.  The default is
# /usr/bin/X11/xauth.
XAuthLocation /usr/bin/X11/xauth
```

Glossary

Word	Definition
Access control list (ACL)	A mechanism that implements access control for a system resource by listing the identities of the system entities that are permitted to access the resource.
Access control service	A security service that provides protection of system resources against unauthorized access. The two basic mechanisms for implementing this service are ACLs and tickets.
Advanced Encryption Standard (AES)	A symmetric encryption algorithm accepted by National Institute of Standards and Technology (NIST) as a result of a public contest. Belgian-authored Rijndael algorithm was accepted as AES, which is generally regarded as a successor to the Data Encryption Standard (DES).
Algorithm	A finite set of step-by-step instructions for a problem-solving or computation procedure, especially one that can be implemented by a computer.
Asymmetric cryptography	Public key cryptography; A modern branch of cryptography in which the algorithms employ a pair of keys (a public key and a private key) and use a different component of the pair for different steps of the algorithm.
Bandwidth	Commonly used to mean the capacity of a communication channel to pass data through the channel in a given amount of time. Usually expressed in bits per second.
Bit	The smallest unit of information storage; a contraction of the term "binary digit"; one of two symbols — "0" (zero) and "1" (one) — that are used to represent binary numbers.
Browser	A client computer program that can retrieve and display information from servers on the World Wide Web.
Brute force	A cryptanalysis technique or other kind of attack method involving an exhaustive procedure that tries all possibilities, one-by-one.
Buffer overflow	A buffer overflow occurs when a program or process tries to store more data in a buffer (temporary data storage area) than it was intended to hold. Since buffers are created to contain a finite amount of data, the extra information - which has to go somewhere - can overflow into adjacent buffers, corrupting or overwriting the valid data held in them. By using a specifically crafted data one can change the execution flow of a target program and cause the execution of unauthorized code.
Byte	A fundamental unit of computer storage; the smallest addressable unit in a computer's architecture. Usually holds one character of information and usually means eight bits.
Cache	Pronounced "cash", a special high-speed storage mechanism. It can be either a reserved section of main memory or an independent high-speed storage device. Two types of caching are commonly used in computers: memory caching and disk caching. The same word is also used to denote a temporary storage of various parameters by network devices, such as DNS cache (used to store name to IP address mapping for a certain time) or ARP cache (used to store associations between hardware or MAC addresses and IP addresses)

Word	Definition
Checksum	A value that is computed by a function that is dependent on the contents of a data object and is stored or transmitted together with the object, for the purpose of detecting changes in the data.
Cipher	A cryptographic algorithm for encryption and decryption.
Client	A system entity that requests and uses a service provided by another system entity, called a "server". In some cases, the server may itself be a client of some other server.
CERT/CC	An organization that studies computer and network INFOSEC in order to provide incident response services to victims of attacks, publish alerts concerning vulnerabilities and threats, and offer other information to help improve computer and network security.
Computer network	A collection of host computers together with the sub-network or inter-network through which they can exchange data.
Corruption	A threat action that undesirably alters system operation by adversely modifying system functions or data.
Cryptanalysis	The mathematical science that deals with analysis of a cryptographic system in order to gain knowledge needed to break or circumvent the protection that the system is designed to provide. In other words, convert the cipher text to plaintext without knowing the key.
Cryptographic algorithm or hash	An algorithm that employs the science of cryptography, including encryption algorithms, cryptographic hash algorithms, digital signature algorithms, and key agreement algorithms.
Cyclic Redundancy Check (CRC)	Sometimes called "cyclic redundancy code". A type of checksum algorithm that is not a cryptographic hash but is used to implement data integrity validation service where accidental changes to data are expected.
Daemon	A program which is often started at the time the system boots and runs continuously without intervention from any of the users on the system. The daemon program forwards the requests to other programs (or processes) as appropriate. The term daemon is a UNIX term, but many other operating systems provide support for daemons, though they're sometimes called other names. Windows, for example, refers to daemons as System Agents and services.
Data Encryption Standard (DES)	A widely used method of data encryption using a private (secret) key. There are 72,000,000,000,000,000 (72 quadrillion) or more possible encryption keys that can be used. For each given message, the key is chosen at random from among this enormous number of keys. Like other private key cryptographic methods, both the sender and the receiver must know and use the same private key. AES succeeded DES as a standard encryption algorithm.
Denial of service	The prevention of authorized access to a system resource or the delaying of system operations and functions.

Word	Definition
Dictionary attack	An attack that uses a brute-force technique of successively trying all the words in some large, exhaustive list. For example, an attack on an authentication service by trying all possible passwords; or an attack on encryption by encrypting some known plaintext phrase with all possible keys so that the key for any given encrypted message containing that phrase may be obtained by lookup.
Diffie-Hellman	A key agreement algorithm published in 1976 by Whitfield Diffie and Martin Hellman. Diffie-Hellman does key establishment, not encryption. However, the key that it produces may be used for encryption, for further key management operations, or for any other cryptography.
Digital certificate	A digital certificate is an electronic "driver's license" that establishes your credentials when doing business or other transactions on the Web. It is issued by a certification authority. It contains your name, a serial number, expiration dates, a copy of the certificate holder's public key (used for encrypting messages and digital signatures), and the digital signature of the certificate-issuing authority so that a recipient can verify that the certificate is real.
Digital Signature Algorithm (DSA)	An asymmetric cryptographic algorithm that produces a digital signature in the form of a pair of large numbers. The signature is computed using rules and parameters such that the identity of the signer and the integrity of the signed data can be verified.
Digital Signature Standard (DSS)	The U.S. Government standard that specifies the Digital Signature Algorithm (DSA), which involves asymmetric cryptography.
Disruption	A circumstance or event that interrupts or prevents the correct operation of system services and functions.
Domain name	For example, as of this writing, the [delete "domain"] name "www.sans.org" locates an Internet address for "sans.org" at IP address 167.216.198.40 and a particular host server named "www.sans.org" at IP address 65.173.218.106. The "org part of the name. The "org" part of the domain name reflects the purpose of the organization or entity (in this example, "organization") and is called the top-level domain name. The "sans" part of the domain name defines the organization or entity and together with the top-level is called the second-level domain name.
Domain Name System (DNS)	The domain name system (DNS) is the way that Internet domain names are located and translated into Internet Protocol (IP) addresses. A domain name is a meaningful and easy-to-remember "handle" for an Internet address.
Encapsulation	The inclusion of one data structure within another structure so that the first data structure is hidden for the time being.
Encryption	Cryptographic transformation of data (called "plaintext") into a form (called "cipher text") that conceals the data's original meaning to prevent it from being known or used.
Ethernet	The most widely-installed LAN technology. Specified in a standard, IEEE 802.3, an Ethernet LAN typically uses coaxial cable or special grades of twisted pair wires. Devices are connected to the cable and compete for access using a CSMA/CD (Carrier-Sense Multiple-Access / Collision Detect) protocol protocol.

Word	Definition
Exposure	A threat action whereby sensitive data is directly released to an unauthorized entity.
Extensible Authentication Protocol (EAP)	A framework that supports multiple, optional authentication mechanisms for PPP, including clear-text passwords, challenge-response, and arbitrary dialog sequences.
File Transfer Protocol (FTP)	A TCP/IP protocol specifying the transfer of text or binary files across the network. FTP uses two communication channels called command and data channels. TCP port 21 is assigned to FTP.
Finger	A protocol to lookup user information on a given host. A UNIX program that takes an e-mail address as input and returns information about the user who owns that e-mail address. On some systems, finger only reports whether the user is currently logged on. Other systems return additional information, such as the user's full name, address, and telephone number. Finger can also be used to retrieve the information on currently logged in users. Of course, the user must first enter this information into the system. Many e-mail programs now have a finger utility built into them.
Fingerprinting	Sending strange packets to a system in order to gauge how it responds to determine the operating system.
Firewall	A logical or physical discontinuity in a network to prevent unauthorized access to data or resources based on a security policy.
Flooding	An attack that attempts to cause a failure in (especially, in the security of) a computer system or other data processing entity by providing more input than the entity can process properly.
Fragmentation	The process of storing a data file in several "chunks" or fragments rather than in a single contiguous sequence of bits in one place on the storage medium. The term is also used to describe the splitting of network packets into smaller chunks to transmit over media supporting only smaller packet sizes.
GNU	GNU is a project to create a UNIX-like operating system that comes with source code that can be copied, modified, and redistributed. The GNU project was started in 1983 by Richard Stallman and others, who formed the Free Software Foundation. The project has produced many system utilities and application software used mainly on other UNIX systems.
Hash function	An algorithm that computes a value based on a data object thereby mapping the data object to a smaller data object.
Hijack attack	A form of active wiretapping in which the attacker seizes control of a previously established communication association.
Honey pot	Programs that simulate one or more network services on a computer's ports. An entire machine containing such services is also called a honeypot. An attacker assumes that vulnerable services are running, which can be used to break into the machine. A honey pot can be used to log access attempts to those ports including the attacker's keystrokes. This could give you advanced warning of a more concerted attack.
Host	A computer system that is accessed by a user from a remote location, or a computer that is connected to a TCP/IP network, including the Internet.

Word	Definition
HTTPS	When used in the first part of a URL (the part that precedes the colon and specifies an access scheme or protocol), this term specifies the use of HTTP enhanced by a security mechanism, which is usually SSL. The communication over HTTPS is encrypted.
Hybrid encryption	An application of cryptography that combines two or more encryption algorithms, particularly a combination of symmetric and asymmetric encryption. Hybrid encryption is used as part of SSL.
Hyperlink	In hypertext or hypermedia, an information object (such as a word, a phrase, or an image; usually highlighted by color or underscoring) that points (indicates how to connect) to related information that is located elsewhere and can be retrieved by activating the link.
Hypertext Markup Language (HTML)	The set of markup symbols or codes inserted in a file intended for display on a World Wide Web browser page.
Hypertext Transfer Protocol (HTTP)	The protocol in the Internet Protocol (IP) family used to transport hypertext documents across an internet. TCP port 80 is assigned to the HTTP protocol.
IMAP	IMAP (Internet Message Access Protocol) allows a client workstation to dynamically access a mailbox on a server host to retrieve mail messages that the server has received, create and manage multiple email folders on the server, search in the remote mail folders and other functions. IMAP is a clear-text protocol.
Internet	A term to describe connecting multiple separate networks together
Internet Protocol (IP)	The method or protocol by which data is sent from one computer to another on the Internet.
Internet Protocol security (IPsec)	A developing standard for security at the network or packet processing layer of network communication. IPSec provides support for integrity, confidentiality and non-repudiation of network communication.
Internet Standard	A specification, approved by the IESG (The Internet Engineering Steering Group)and published as an RFC, that is stable and well-understood, is technically competent, has multiple, independent, and interoperable implementations with substantial operational experience, enjoys significant public support, and is recognizably useful in some or all parts of the Internet.
Intranet	A computer network, especially one based on Internet technology, that an organization uses for its own internal, and usually private, purposes and that is closed to outsiders.
Intrusion detection System (IDS)	A security management system for computers and networks. An IDS gathers and analyzes information from various areas within a computer or a network to identify possible security breaches, which include both intrusions (attacks from outside the organization) and misuse (attacks from within the organization).
IP address	A computer's inter-network address that is assigned for use by the Internet Protocol and other protocols. An IP version 4 address is written as a series of four 8-bit numbers separated by periods.
IP flood	A denial of service (DoS) attack that sends a host more ICMP (such as "ping"), UDP or TCP (such as SYN) packets than the protocol implementation can handle.

Word	Definition
IP spoofing	The technique of making network communication look as if it originated at a different IP address.
Kerberos	A system developed at the Massachusetts Institute of Technology that depends on passwords and symmetric cryptography(DES) to implement ticket-based, peer entity authentication service and access control service distributed in a client-server network environment.
Kernel	The essential center of a computer operating system, the core that provides basic services for all other parts of the operating system. A synonym is nucleus. A kernel can be contrasted with a shell, the outermost part of an operating system that interacts with user commands. Kernel and shell are terms used more frequently in UNIX and some other operating systems than in IBM mainframe systems or Windows systems
Layer 2 Tunneling Protocol (L2TP)	An extension of the Point-to-Point Tunneling Protocol used by an Internet service provider to enable the operation of a virtual private network over the Internet.
MAC address	A physical address; a numeric value that uniquely identifies that network device interface from every other device on the planet. The MAC address is given to each network adapter card. The SAN fibre-interface version of the MAC address is the World Wide Name (WWN).
Trojan	Software (e.g., Trojan horse) that appears to perform a useful or desirable function, but actually gains unauthorized access to system resources or tricks a user into executing other malicious code.
Malware (Malicious Software)	A generic term for a number of different types of malicious code, such as viruses (self-replicating code), worms, Trojans, logic bombs, etc.
Masquerade attack	A type of attack in which one system entity illegitimately poses as (assumes the identity of) another entity.
Netmask (network mask)	32-bit number indicating the range of IP addresses residing on a single IP network/subnet/supernet. This specification displays network masks as hexadecimal numbers. For example, the network mask for a class C IP network is displayed as 0xffffff00. Such a mask is often displayed elsewhere in the literature as 255.255.255.0.
Network Address Translation	The translation of an Internet Protocol address used within one network to a different IP address known within another network. One network is designated the inside network and the other is the outside.
Null session	Known as Anonymous Logon, it is a way of letting an anonymous user retrieve information such as user names and shares over the network or connect without authentication to a Windows machine. It is used by applications such as explorer.exe to enumerate shares on remote Windows servers.
Octet	A sequence of eight bits. An octet is an eight-bit byte.
One-way encryption	Irreversible transformation of plaintext to cipher text, such that the plaintext cannot be recovered from the cipher text by other than exhaustive procedures even if the cryptographic key is known. It is used for the same purpose as a hash function.
One-way function	A (mathematical) function, f, which is easy to compute, but which for a general value y in the range, it is computationally difficult to find a value x in the domain such that f(x) = y. There may be a few values of y for which finding x is not computationally difficult.

Word	Definition
OpenSSH	OpenSSH is a free open-source implementation of SSH client and server, which runs on many platforms. OpenSSH supports all the SSH protocol versions that commercial SSH supports and is fully interoperable with other SSH implementations.
Packet	A piece of a message transmitted over a packet-switching network. One of the key features of a packet is that it contains the destination address in addition to the data. In IP networks, packets are often called datagrams.
Pageant	This is an SSH authentication agent (included with PuTTY SSH client) that will keep your private keys in memory so you do not have to enter your pass phrase in every time you log in to a server.
Password sniffing	Passive wiretapping, usually on a local area network, to gain knowledge of passwords. Clear-text protocols such as telnet and FTP can be subject to password sniffing.
Penetration	Gaining unauthorized logical access to sensitive data by circumventing a system's protections.
Plaintext	Ordinary readable text before being encrypted into ciphertext or after being decrypted.
Plink	This is a command line interface to PuTTY that can be used to create secure connections to SSH servers in scripts.
Point-to-Point Protocol (PPP)	A protocol for communication between two computers using a serial interface, typically a personal computer connected by phone line to a server. It packages your computer's TCP/IP packets and forwards them to the server where they can actually be put on the Internet or any other untrusted TCP/IP network.
Point-to-Point Tunneling Protocol (PPTP)	A protocol (set of communication rules) that allows corporations to extend their own corporate network through private "tunnels" over the public Internet or any other untrusted TCP/IP network.
Port scan	A port scan is a series of messages sent by someone attempting to break into a computer to learn which computer network services, each associated with a "well-known" port number, the computer provides. Port scanning, a favorite approach of computer crackers, gives the assailant an idea where to probe for weaknesses. Essentially, a port scan consists of sending a message to each port, one at a time. The kind of response received indicates whether the port is used and can therefore be probed for weakness.
Pretty Good Privacy (PGP)™	Trademark of PGP, Inc., referring to a computer program (and related protocols) that uses public key and symmetric cryptography to provide data security for electronic mail and other applications on the Internet and on the host level.
Private addressing	IANA has set aside three address ranges for use by private or non-Internet connected networks. This is referred to as Private Address Space and is defined in RFC 1918. The reserved address blocks are: 10.0.0.0 to 10.255.255.255 (10/8 prefix) 172.16.0.0 to 172.31.255.255 (172.16/12 prefix) 192.168.0.0 to 192.168.255.255 (192.168/16 prefix)

Word	Definition
Promiscuous mode	When a machine reads all packets off the network, regardless of who they are addressed to. This is used by network administrators to diagnose network problems, but also by unsavory characters who are trying to eavesdrop on network traffic (which might contain passwords or other information).
Protocol	A formal specification for communicating; a special set of pre-defined rules that end points in a telecommunication connection use when they communicate. Protocols exist at several levels in a telecommunication connection.
PSCP	This is a command line scp client included with the PuTTY suite.
PSFTP	This is a command line sftp client included with the PuTTY suite. PSFTP will only work on SSH servers that support SSH version 2 since the SFTP protocol is only supported there.
Public key	The publicly-disclosed component of a pair of cryptographic keys used for asymmetric cryptography.
Public key Encryption	The popular synonym for "asymmetric cryptography".
Public Key infrastructure (PKI)	A PKI (public key infrastructure) enables users of a basically unsecured public network such as the Internet to securely and privately exchange data through the use of a public and a private cryptographic key pair that is obtained and shared through a trusted authority. The public key infrastructure provides for a digital certificate that can identify an individual or an organization and directory services that can store, issue, manage and, when necessary, revoke the certificates.
Public key forward secrecy (PFS)	For a key agreement protocol based on asymmetric cryptography, the property that ensures that a session key derived from a set of long-term public and private keys will not be compromised if one of the private keys is compromised in the future.
PuTTY	PuTTY is an open source Windows SSH and telnet client distributed under the MIT license and maintained by Simon Tatham. The package contains all of the necessary components required to connect to a machine running OpenSSH and runs on all versions of Windows starting at Windows 95.
PuTTYgen	This is a key generation utility that will create RSA1, DSA and RSA public/private key-pairs for authentication with all of the PuTTY components.
PuTTYtel	This is a telnet only client, included with the PuTTY package.
Rivest-Shamir-Adleman (RSA)	An algorithm for asymmetric cryptography, invented in 1977 by Ron Rivest, Adi Shamir, and Leonard Adleman.
Rootkit	A collection of tools (programs) that a hacker uses to mask intrusion and maintain administrator-level access to a computer or computer network after the compromise. Rootkits are most commonly seen on UNIX/Linux machines.
S/Key	A security mechanism that uses a cryptographic hash function to generate a sequence of 64-bit, one-time passwords for remote user login. The client generates a one-time password by applying the MD4 cryptographic hash function multiple times to the user's secret key. For each successive authentication of the user, the number of hash applications is reduced by one.

Word	Definition
Scavenging	Searching through data residue (such as a swap file or unallocated disk space) in a system to gain unauthorized knowledge of sensitive data.
Secure Shell (SSH)	A protocol for encrypted communication between two computers over a TCP/IP network, typically using TCP port 22. Also, an implementation of a telnet-like program utilizing the SSH protocol.
Secure Sockets Layer (SSL)	A protocol developed by Netscape for transmitting private documents via the Internet. SSL works by using public key cryptography together with symmetric cryptography to encrypt data that's transferred over the SSL connection. The most common application of SSL is secure web access (HTTPS).
Security policy	A set of rules and practices that specify or regulate how a system or organization provides security services to protect sensitive and critical system resources.
Server	A system entity that provides a service in response to requests from other system entities called clients.
Session hijacking	Taking over a session that someone else has established.
Session key	In the context of symmetric encryption, a key that is temporary or is used for a relatively short period of time. Usually, a session key is used for a defined period of communication between two computers, such as for the duration of a single connection or transaction set, or the key is used in an application that protects relatively large amounts of data and, therefore, needs to be re-keyed frequently.
Shadow password files	A system file in which encrypted user passwords are stored on a UNIX system so that they are only available to the system administrator, i.e. root user.
Shell	A UNIX term for the interactive user interface with an operating system. The shell is the layer of programming that understands and executes the commands a user enters. In some systems, the shell is called a command interpreter. A shell usually implies an interface with a command syntax (think of the DOS operating system and its "C:>" prompts and user commands such as "dir" and "edit"), but a graphical user interface might also be called a "shell".
Signals analysis	Gaining indirect knowledge of communicated data by monitoring and analyzing a signal that is emitted by a system and that contains the data but is not intended to communicate the data.
SMTP	Simple Mail Transfer Protocol (SMTP) is used to tranfser email from the sender to receiver. Usually, a workstation connects to an email server over SMTP and transfers the email. Then, the server uses SMTP to send email to its destination. SMTP is a clear-text protocol.
Sniffing	A synonym for "passive wiretapping".
Social engineering	An euphemism for non-technical or low-technology means — such as lies, impersonation, tricks, bribes, blackmail, and threats — used to mislead personnel in order to get access to information systems and other resources.
Software	Computer programs (which are stored in and executed by computer hardware) and associated data (which also is stored in the hardware) that may be dynamically written or modified during execution.

Word	Definition
Source port	The port that a host uses to connect to a server. It is usually a number greater than or equal to 1024. It is randomly generated and is different each time a connection is made.
Spam	Electronic junk mail or junk newsgroup postings.
Split key	A cryptographic key that is divided into two or more separate data items that individually convey no knowledge of the whole key that results from combining the items. Split key is commonly used to avoid giving any single person complete control over the encryption key.
Spoof	Attempt by an unauthorized entity to gain access to a system by posing as an authorized user.
Steganography	Methods of hiding the existence of a message or other data. This is different than cryptography, which hides the meaning of a message but does not hide the message itself. An example of a steganographic method is "invisible" ink.
Subnet mask (netmask)	A subnet mask (or number) is used to determine the number of bits used for the subnet and host portions of the address. In IPv4 networks, the mask is a 32-bit value that uses one-bits for the network and subnet portions and zero-bits for the host portion.
Switched network	A communications network, such as the public switched telephone network, in which any user may be connected to any other user through the use of message, circuit, or packet switching and control devices. Any network providing switched communications service. The term is also used to mean a "switch-based LAN" (as opposed to a hub-based shared LAN).
Symmetric cryptography	A branch of cryptography involving algorithms that use the same key for two different steps of the algorithm (such as encryption and decryption, or signature creation and signature verification). Symmetric cryptography is sometimes called "secret-key cryptography" (versus public key cryptography) because the entities that share the key must keep it secret.
Symmetric key	A cryptographic key that is used in a symmetric cryptographic algorithm.
SYN flood	A denial of service attack that sends a host more TCP SYN packets (request to synchronize sequence numbers, used when opening a connection) than the protocol implementation can handle. Unlike other types of flooding (such as ICMP or UDP flood) a SYN flood exhausts target host resources (in the form of a kernel connection table) and not the network bandwidth, allowing it to deal higher damage with a smaller number of packets.
System Security Officer (SSO)	A person responsible for enforcement or administration of the security policy that applies to the system.
Tamper	To deliberately alter a system's logic, data, or control information to cause the system to perform unauthorized functions or services.
TCP Wrappers	A software package which can be used to restrict access to certain network services based on the source of the connection on UNIX systems; a simple tool to monitor and control incoming network traffic.

Word	Definition
TCP/IP	A synonym for "Internet Protocol Suite", in which the Transmission Control Protocol and the Internet Protocol are important parts. TCP/IP is the basic communication language or protocol of the Internet. It can also be used as a communications protocol in a private network (either an intranet or an extranet).
TELNET	A TCP-based, application-layer, clear-text (i.e. unencrypted) Internet Standard protocol for remote login from one host to another.
Threat	A potential for violation of security, which exists when there is a circumstance, capability, action, or event that could breach security and cause harm.
Threat vector	The method a threat uses to get to the target.
Transmission Control Protocol (TCP)	A set of rules (protocol) used along with the Internet Protocol to send data in the form of message units between computers over the Internet. While IP takes care of handling the actual delivery of the data, TCP takes care of keeping track of the individual units of data (called packets) that a message is divided into for efficient routing through the Internet. Whereas the IP protocol deals only with packets, TCP enables two hosts to establish a connection and exchange streams of data. TCP guarantees delivery of data and also guarantees that packets will be delivered in the same order in which they were sent.
Transport Layer Security (TLS)	A protocol that ensures privacy between communicating applications and their users on the Internet. When a server and client communicate, TLS ensures that no third party may eavesdrop or tamper with any message. TLS is the successor to the Secure Sockets Layer (SSL).
Triple DES	A block cipher, based on DES, that transforms each 64-bit plaintext block by applying the data encryption algorithm three successive times, using either two or three different 56-bit keys, for an effective key length of 112 or 168 bits.
Triple-wrapped	S/MIME usage: Data that has been signed with a digital signature, and then encrypted, and then signed again.
Trojan horse	A computer program that appears to have a useful function, but also has a hidden and potentially malicious function that evades security mechanisms, sometimes by exploiting legitimate authorizations of a system entity that invokes the program.
Tunnel	A communication channel created in a computer network by encapsulating a communication protocol's data packets in (on top of) a second protocol that normally would be carried above, or at the same layer as, the first one. Most often, a tunnel is a logical point-to-point link — i.e., an OSI layer 2 connection — created by encapsulating the layer 2 protocol in a transport protocol (such as TCP), in a network or inter-network layer protocol (such as IP), or in another link layer protocol. Tunneling can move data between computers that use a protocol not supported by the network connecting them.
Uniform Resource Locator (URL)	The global address of documents and other resources on the World Wide Web. The first part of the address indicates what protocol to use, and the second part specifies the IP address or the domain name where the resource is located. For example, http://www.pcwebopedia.com/index.html.

Word	Definition
UNIX	A popular multi-user, multitasking operating system developed at Bell Labs in the early 1970s. Created by just a handful of programmers, UNIX was designed to be a small, flexible system used exclusively by programmers, but quickly grew to worldwide acceptance.
User	A person, organization entity, or automated process that accesses a system, whether authorized to do so or not.
User Datagram Protocol (UDP)	A communications protocol that, like TCP, runs on top of IP networks. Unlike TCP/IP, UDP/IP provides very few error recovery services, offering instead a direct way to send and receive datagrams over an IP network. It's used primarily for broadcasting messages over a network. UDP uses the Internet Protocol to get a datagram from one computer to another but does not divide a message into packets (datagrams) and reassemble it at the other end. Specifically, UDP doesn't provide sequencing of the packets that the data arrives in so that the messages might arrive out of order.
Virtual Private Network (VPN)	A restricted-use, logical (i.e., artificial or simulated) computer network that is constructed from the system resources of a relatively public, physical (i.e., real) network (such as the Internet), often by using encryption (located at hosts or gateways), and often by tunneling links of the virtual network across the real network. For example, if a corporation has LANs at several different sites, each connected to the Internet by a firewall, the corporation could create a VPN by (a) using encrypted tunnels to connect from firewall to firewall across the Internet and (b) not allowing any other traffic through the firewalls. A VPN is generally less expensive to build and operate than a dedicated real network, because the virtual network shares the cost of system resources with other users of the real network.
Virus	A hidden, self-replicating section of computer software, usually malicious logic, that propagates by infecting — i.e., inserting a copy of itself into and becoming part of — another program. A virus cannot run by itself; it requires that its host program be run to make the virus active.
Vulnerability	A flaw or weakness in a system's design, implementation, or operation and management that could be exploited to violate the system's security policy.
Web server	A software process that runs on a host computer connected to the Internet to respond to HTTP requests for documents from client web browsers.
WinSCP, WinSCP2	WinSCP and WinSCP2 are free Windows implementations of a secure copy program. They allow to easily and securely copy files between computers, such as from a UNIX ssh or OpenSSH server to a Windows workstation.
Wiretapping	Monitoring and recording data that is flowing between two points in a communication system.
World Wide Web ("the Web", WWW, W3)	The global, hypermedia-based collection of information and services that is available on Internet servers and is accessed by browsers using Hypertext Transfer Protocol and other information retrieval mechanisms.
Worm	A computer program that can run independently, can propagate a complete working version of itself onto other hosts on a network, and may consume computer resources destructively.
Wrap	To use cryptography to provide data confidentiality service for a data object.

References:

- Cotse Dictionaries and Encyclopedias, `http://real.cotse.com/cgi-bin/Dict`
- Google, `http://www.google.com/`
- Webopedia Online Dictionary for Computer and Internet Terms, `http://www.pcwebopedia.com`
- Telecom Glossary, **`http://www.its.bldrdoc.gov/projects/telecomglossary2000`**
- Network Glossary, `http://www.clock.org/~jss/glossary/index.html`
- Hal Pomeranz, `http://www.deer-run.com`

Added references by Anton Chuvakin

- RFC 2828, Internet Security Glossary, May 2000, `http://www.ietf.org/rfc/rfc2828.txt`
- The SecurityWatch.com glossary, Ubizen, `http://www.securitywatch.com/edu/ency/1111.html`
- The NSA Glossary of Terms Used in Security and Intrusion Detection, `http://www.sans.org/newlook/resources/glossary.html`
- The glossary of Lexias, Inc., `http://www.lexias.com/glossary1.html`
- Cisco's Internetworking Terms and Acronyms, `http://www.cisco.com/univercd/cc/td/doc/cisintwk/ita/index.html`
- Whatis?com, `http://whatis.techtarget.com`

RSA Security's glossary, `http://www.rsasecurity.com/rsalabs/faq/B.html`

Anne & Lynn Wheeler's security glossary, `http://www.garlic.com/~lynn/secgloss.html`

The ABC of computer security, Sophos Inc., `http://www.sophos.com/virusinfo/whitepapers/abc.html`